The **Ultimate** Guide
SHARK

Miles
KeLLy

First published in 2017 by
Miles Kelly Publishing Ltd, Harding's Barn,
Bardfield End Green, Thaxted, Essex,
CM6 3PX, UK

2 4 6 8 10 9 7 5 3 1

Author Barbara Taylor

Publishing Director Belinda Gallagher
Creative Director Jo Brewer
Editorial Director Rosie Neave
Design Manager Simon Lee
Image Manager Liberty Newton
Indexer Marie Lorimer
Production Elizabeth Collins,
Caroline Kelly
Reprographics Stephan Davis,
Jennifer Cozens

ISBN 978-1-78617-245-7

Printed in China

British Library Cataloguing-in-Publication Data
A catalogue record for this book is available
from the British Library

Made with paper from a sustainable forest

www.mileskelly.net

ACKNOWLEDGEMENTS

The publishers would like to thank Stuart
Jackson-Carter for the cover and acetate
features artwork

All other artworks are from the Miles Kelly
Artwork Bank

The publishers would like to thank the following
sources for the use of their photographs:

Key: t = top, b = bottom, c = centre, l = left,
r = right

Main pages:
Alamy 40(b) Doug Perrine/Alamy Stock Photo
Ardea.com 28(t) Valerie & Ron Taylor;
62(b) Valerie & Ron Taylor
Dreamstime.com 48(t) Naluphoto
FLPA 5(b) Jeffrey Rotman/Biosphoto; 38(t) &
45(t) Fred Bavendam/Minden Pictures, (b)
Norbert Wu/Minden Pictures; 46(t) Norbert
Probst/Imagebroker
Fotolia.com 61(t)
Getty Images 20(b) Luciano Candisani/
Minden Pictures; 21(t) Tui De Roy/Minden
Pictures; 30 Brian J. Skerry
Glow Images 10(t) Imagebroker
Image Quest Marine 49(b) Andy Murch;
55(b) Image Quest Marine
Naturepl.com 7(tl) Doug Perrine; (tr) Michele
Westmorland; 21(br) Jeff Rotman; 29(t) Doug
Perrine; (b) Jeff Rotman; 37(t) Florian Graner;
42(t) Chris and Monique Fallows; 51(b) Chris
and Monique Fallows; 61(b) Alex
Mustard/2020Vision

OceanwideImages.com 4(t) C & M Fallows;
22(t) Andy Murch; 40(t) Justin Gilligan
Photoshot 14(b) Oceans Image
SeaPics.com 31(b) Doug Perrine
Shark Trust 62(t)
Shutterstock.com back cover (tl) James A
Dawson, (cl) Jim Agronick, (tr) Matt9122,
(cr) gfdunt; 2(bl) cbpix; 3(br) Dray van Beeck;
4(b) nicolasvoisin44; 5(t) Krzysztof Odziomek;
6(b) Greg Amptman; 7(b) frantisekhojdysz;
10(b) Fiona Ayerst; 12(t) cbpix;
14(t) NatalieJean; 18(t) Dray van Beeck,
(b) Matt9122; 19(b) Pommeyrol Vincent;
20(t) Matt9122; 21(bl) Photon75; 22(b) A
Cotton Photo; 23(t) Dudarev Mikhail;
26(t) Brandelet; 31(t) Greg Amptman;
38(b) iliuta goean; 39(b) Sergey Dubrov;
47(b) Fiona Ayerst; 48(b) Ian Scott;
49(t) Micha Rosenwirth; 52(b) Durden Images;
53(t) Ethan Daniels; 55(c) Greg Amptman;
58(b) Gustavo Miguel Fernandes;
59(t) kbrowne41, (b) Greg Amptman

Acetate feature pages:
Skeleton and muscles 8(tr) Brian J. Skerry/
National Geographic Creative, (bl) David
Jenkins/robertharding/REX/Shutterstock,
(br) Andy Murch/OceanwideImages.com;
acetate (bl) Carver Mostardi/Alamy Stock
Photo, (c) nitrogenic.com/Shutterstock.com,
(br) Sandra Raredon/Smithsonian Institution;
9(bl) Gary Corbett/Alamy Stock Photo
Gills and breathing 16(cl) Sue Daly/
naturepl.com, (tr) Shane Gross/Shutterstock.
com, (br) Alex Mustard/2020VISION/naturepl.
com; *acetate* (tr) Mark Conlin/SeaPics.com,
(bl) Kelvin Aitken/ VWPics /Alamy Stock
Photo, (c) by wildestanimal/Getty, (br) Kike
Calvo/VWPICS/Alamy Stock Photo; 17(tr)
Nigel Marsh, (br) Jeff Rotman/naturepl.com
Teeth and digestion 24(cl) Suzanne Lowe/
Newspix/REX/Shutterstock, (tr) Jeff Rotman/
Alamy Stock Photo, (br) Justin Duggan/
Newspix/REX/Shutterstock; *acetate* (c)
WaterFrame/Alamy Stock Photo, (br) Elsa
Hoffmann/Shutterstock.com, (ctl) Frans
Lanting/Frans Lanting Stock/National
Geographic Creative, (cbl) Jeff Rotman/Getty
Images, (cr) Getty Images, 25(br) Jeff Rotman/
Alamy Stock Photo
Eggs and babies 32(bl) Doug Perrine/
SeaPics.com, (tr) D R Schrichte/SeaPics.com,
(br) Fred Bavendam/Minden Pictures/FLPA;
acetate (br) Mark Conlin/SeaPics.com,
(t) Michele Hall/SeaPics.com, 33(bl) Paul
Nicklen/National Geographic Creative,
(br) Steve Trewhella/FLPA
Inside a ray 56(cl) Jonathan Bird/Getty
Images, (c) J. Henning Buchholz/Shutterstock.
com, (br) Richard Herrmann/Minden Pictures/
FLPA; *acetate* (t) Todd Aki/Getty Images,
(bl) Paul Souders/Getty Images, (br) Doug
Perrine/SeaPics.com
Top Ten Deadliest Sharks poster:
Shutterstock.com Bull shark Ian Scott; Great
white shark Jim Agronick; Oceanic whitetip
shark Dray van Beeck; Blue shark FAUP;
Blacktip reef shark cbpix; Sand tiger shark
Clay S. Turner; (bg) Peshkov Daniil;
(star & panel texture) Redshinestudio
Dreamstime Tiger shark Naluphoto
Naturepl.com Great Hammerhead shark and
Shortfin Mako shark Brandon Cole;
Narrowhead shark Doug Perrine

All other photographs are from: Corel,
digitalSTOCK, digitalvision, dreamstime.com,
Fotolia.com, iStock/Getty, PhotoDisc

Every effort has been made to acknowledge
the source and copyright holder of each
picture. Miles Kelly Publishing apologizes for
any unintentional errors or omissions.

Contents

ALL ABOUT SHARKS

What is a shark?	4
Records and statistics	4
Big and small	5
Shallows to the deep	6
Tropics to Poles	7
Reef sharks	7

HOW SHARKS WORK

Shark profile: Skeleton and muscles	**8**
On the move	10
Swimming skills	10
Fast sharks	11
Long-distance travel	11
Shark fins	12
Shark tails	12
Shark shapes	13
Sandpaper skin	13
Staying safe	14
In disguise	14
A look inside	15
Shark profile: Gills and breathing	**16**
Eyes and vision	18
Sensing smells	18
Touch and taste	19
Hearing sounds	19
The sixth sense	20

Blacktip reef sharks 49
Spinner sharks 49
Night sharks 50
River sharks 50
Hammerhead sharks 51

SHARK RELATIVES

Shark relatives 52
Rays 52
Electric rays 53
Stingrays 53
Skates 54
Guitarfish 54
Sawfish 55
Chimaeras 55
Shark profile:
   Inside a ray 56

SHARKS AND PEOPLE

Dangerous or not? 58
Attacks and survival 58
Studying sharks 59
Observation 59
Early sharks 60
Shark fossils 60
Sharks in trouble 61
Endangered species 61
Saving sharks 62

Index 63

Smart sharks 20
Food and feeding 21
Teeth and jaws 21
Going hunting 22
Filter feeding 23
Scavenging food 23
Shark profile:
   Teeth and digestion 24

LIFE CYCLES

Loners and groups 26
Sending messages 26
Meeting and mating 27
Male and female sharks 28
Laying eggs 28
Giving birth 29
Newborn sharks 29
Growing up 30
Friends and enemies 31
Shark profile:
   Eggs and babies 32

SHARK FAMILIES

Types of shark 34
Angelsharks 35
Sawsharks 35
Dogfish sharks 36
Greenland sharks 36
Lanternsharks 37
Cookie-cutter sharks 37
Bullhead sharks 38
Carpet sharks 38
Whale sharks 39
Nurse sharks 39
Wobbegongs 40
Mackerel sharks 40
Goblin sharks 41
Megamouth sharks 41
Sand tiger sharks 42
Thresher sharks 42
Basking sharks 43
Great white sharks 43
Mako sharks 44
Porbeagle sharks 44
Catsharks 45
Swellsharks 45
Houndsharks 46
Weasel sharks 46
Requiem sharks 47
Blue sharks 47
Tiger sharks 48
Bull sharks 48

What is a shark?

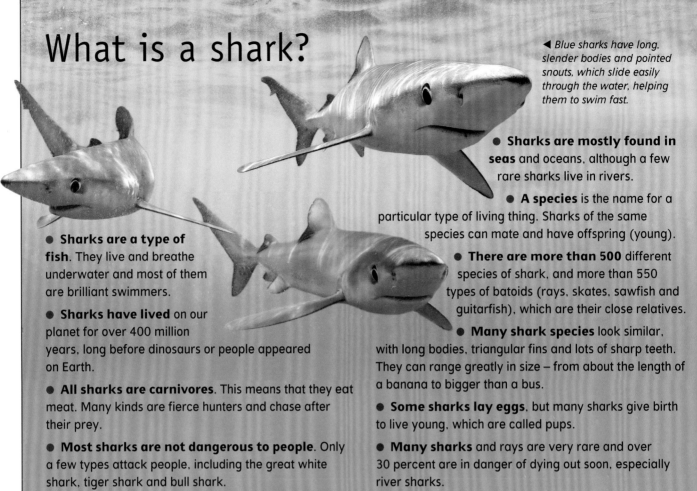

◀ Blue sharks have long, slender bodies and pointed snouts, which slide easily through the water, helping them to swim fast.

● **Sharks are a type of fish**. They live and breathe underwater and most of them are brilliant swimmers.

● **Sharks have lived** on our planet for over 400 million years, long before dinosaurs or people appeared on Earth.

● **All sharks are carnivores**. This means that they eat meat. Many kinds are fierce hunters and chase after their prey.

● **Most sharks are not dangerous to people**. Only a few types attack people, including the great white shark, tiger shark and bull shark.

● **Sharks are mostly found in seas** and oceans, although a few rare sharks live in rivers.

● **A species** is the name for a particular type of living thing. Sharks of the same species can mate and have offspring (young).

● **There are more than 500** different species of shark, and more than 550 types of batoids (rays, skates, sawfish and guitarfish), which are their close relatives.

● **Many shark species** look similar, with long bodies, triangular fins and lots of sharp teeth. They can range greatly in size – from about the length of a banana to bigger than a bus.

● **Some sharks lay eggs**, but many sharks give birth to live young, which are called pups.

● **Many sharks** and rays are very rare and over 30 percent are in danger of dying out soon, especially river sharks.

Records and statistics

● **The most widespread shark** is the blue shark, found in most of the world's seas and oceans.

● **The brightest luminescent shark** is the cookie-cutter. Its glow is as bright as a reading lamp.

● **The sharks with the flattest bodies** are wobbegong sharks and angelsharks.

● **The bigeye thresher shark** has the biggest eyes in relation to its body size.

● **Shortfin makos** make the highest leaps: They can jump more than 5 m out of the water.

● **The fussiest eaters** of the shark world are bullhead sharks. The diet of some bullheads consists of sea urchins and nothing else.

● **The common thresher shark** has the longest tail compared to its body size. The tail can be up to half of the shark's body length.

● **The fastest shark** is the shortfin mako shark, which reaches speeds of over 50 km/h.

● **The shark with the most poisonous** flesh is the Greenland shark.

● **The longest lifespans** for sharks range from 75 years for the spiny dogfish to perhaps over 100 years for the whale shark and Greenland shark.

▼ A thresher shark's tail is up to 1.5 m long. When flicked from side to side, the tail makes a powerful weapon for catching prey.

DID YOU KNOW?

Thresher sharks are the second most threatened shark family, after angelsharks.

Big and small

● **The biggest shark** ever, *Megalodon*, is now extinct. This means the species has completely died out. Scientists think *Megalodon* may have weighed almost twice as much as a whale shark.

● **The whale shark** is the biggest living shark. It can measure over 12 m in length – that's as long as two buses end-to-end.

● **Whale sharks** are gentle fish that feed by filtering tiny food particles from the water.

● **The biggest hunting shark** is the great white. Its mouth can measure up to 1.2 m wide – big enough to swallow a seal whole.

▼ *The gigantic whale shark is the biggest fish in the world.*

● **Most sharks** are medium-sized, measuring 1–3 m in length.

● **The average size** for a shark is very similar to the average size of a human.

● **Although some types** are small, most sharks are still bigger than other kinds of fish.

▼ *Pygmy sharks are no more than 27 cm long.*

● **The smallest types** are the spined pygmy shark and the dwarf lanternshark. The dwarf lanternshark is only about 16–19 cm long.

● **The giant lanternshark** is four times longer than these tiny sharks. It grows up to 86 cm long.

● **Smaller sharks** usually feed near the ocean floor, while larger sharks feed in the middle of the ocean and near the surface, where they can hunt larger prey, such as seals.

● **The hammerhead shark** with the biggest 'hammer' is the winghead shark. The width of its hammer is about 50 percent of its body length.

● **The biggest ray** is the oceanic manta ray, which is usually about 7 m wide and 7 m long (including the tail). The biggest mantas are nearly 9 m wide.

Shallows to the deep

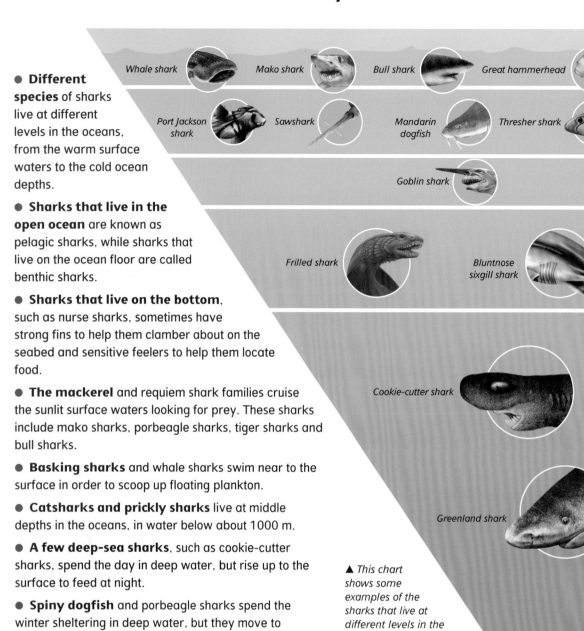

● **Different species** of sharks live at different levels in the oceans, from the warm surface waters to the cold ocean depths.

● **Sharks that live in the open ocean** are known as pelagic sharks, while sharks that live on the ocean floor are called benthic sharks.

● **Sharks that live on the bottom**, such as nurse sharks, sometimes have strong fins to help them clamber about on the seabed and sensitive feelers to help them locate food.

● **The mackerel** and requiem shark families cruise the sunlit surface waters looking for prey. These sharks include mako sharks, porbeagle sharks, tiger sharks and bull sharks.

● **Basking sharks** and whale sharks swim near to the surface in order to scoop up floating plankton.

● **Catsharks and prickly sharks** live at middle depths in the oceans, in water below about 1000 m.

● **A few deep-sea sharks**, such as cookie-cutter sharks, spend the day in deep water, but rise up to the surface to feed at night.

● **Spiny dogfish** and porbeagle sharks spend the winter sheltering in deep water, but they move to shallow waters near the coast in spring and autumn.

● **Portuguese sharks** have been found at depths of nearly 3700 m below the sea's surface. They live at such great depths that scientists know little about them.

● **Cold water sharks**, such as the frilled shark and the goblin shark, often live in very deep water.

● **Many deep-sea sharks**, such as the dwarf shark and the velvet belly lantern shark, glow in the dark to help them find food in deep, dark water.

● **Gulper sharks** and other deep-sea sharks have huge green eyes to help them see in dark and gloomy waters.

● **Living on the deep-sea floor** are sixgill, sevengill and sleeper sharks. They eat food that sinks down from the surface of the sea.

▲ This chart shows some examples of the sharks that live at different levels in the oceans.

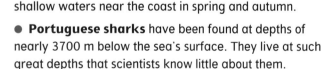

▲ Sixgill sharks have large eyes to help them capture as much light as possible in deep, dark waters. This shark is only a pup.

Tropics to Poles

● **More species of sharks** live in warm or hot tropical oceans than in cold polar waters.

● **Most of the top shark hunters**, such as blue sharks or oceanic whitetip sharks, thrive in tropical oceans where the water is warmer than 21°C.

● **Other tropical species** that prefer to swim and hunt in warm waters include reef sharks, nurse sharks and whale sharks.

● **Temperate water sharks**, such as mako sharks, basking sharks and horn sharks, live in cooler waters, with temperatures ranging from 10–20°C.

● **The great white shark** lives in temperate waters, but also swims in tropical oceans and warm seas, such as the Mediterranean Sea.

▼ *Greenland sharks live in the cold waters of the North Atlantic Ocean – further north than almost any other shark.*

● **Where water temperatures** are lower than 10°C, fewer sharks are able to survive and they move more slowly.

● **Cold water sharks** include the smoothhound shark, spiny dogfish, porbeagle shark and sleeper sharks.

● **The porbeagle shark** lives in waters with temperatures as low as 2°C, but is still able to chase fish at the surface of the sea.

● **The Greenland shark** is the only shark that survives under the polar ice in the North Atlantic Ocean.

● **Although the Greenland shark** grows slowly, it reaches a large size of over 6.5 m, and may live for 100 years or more.

▶ *Scalloped hammerhead sharks swim in warm temperate and tropical oceans all over the world. They migrate northwards in summer, but return to warmer tropical waters in the winter.*

Reef sharks

● **Many species of shark** live on or around coral reefs because of the warm waters, and the variety of food and places to shelter.

● **Reef sharks** often patrol along the edge of the reef, ready to catch day-hunting fish returning to the safety of the reef at night.

● **The names of some sharks**, such as grey reef sharks and blacktip reef sharks reflect their habitat.

● **Many reef sharks** are very curious. They will swim close to divers, or steal fish from the spears of fishermen hunting underwater.

▼ *Caribbean reef sharks are the most common sharks on the reefs in the Caribbean Sea. They are large, reaching lengths of 2–3 m.*

● **Silvertip sharks** are bold and aggressive reef sharks. Adults often have a lot of scars from fights with other sharks and they sometimes attack human divers.

● **Whitetip reef sharks** rest during the day in caves or under rocks, and hunt for fish in packs at night. Their tough skin helps to protect them from the sharp coral.

● **Like many sharks**, reef sharks have dark backs and paler undersides. This helps to camouflage them from predators or prey, either looking down at the dark water below them, or up towards the lighter water at the sea's surface.

● **The blacknose shark** is a small reef shark, which often swims with other blacknose sharks in large schools. This shark is a fast swimmer and feeds on small fish, such as anchovies.

● **Reef sharks** do not usually make long migration journeys as they have a plentiful supply of food, and places to mate and rear their young all year round.

● **Grey reef sharks** use body language, such as arching their backs and pointing their front fins down, to warn rivals to keep away from their patch of coral reef.

Skeleton and muscles

A shark's skeleton is made of cartilage. This tough, gristly, rubbery substance is lighter and more flexible than bone. It supports the shark's body, protects its organs and provides a strong framework for muscles to pull against to move the body. Joints at different parts of the skeleton allow a complex range of movements.

Most fish have skeletons made of rigid bone instead of bendy cartilage. They are called bony fish, while sharks (and their relatives, rays and skates) are called cartilaginous fish. A shark's spine and jaws are reinforced with hard crystals of minerals such as calcium, making these parts stronger for extra support and protection.

For its size, a shark's body contains twice as much muscle as the human body. This makes sharks powerful swimmers and helps some sharks to travel long distances through the oceans. A shark's muscles also help to move its jaws, throat and gills, keep its heart beating, and push food, waste and blood through its body. The cardiac muscle in a shark's heart works automatically all the time, tirelessly keeping the shark alive.

Sharks have two types of muscle for moving their skeleton – red muscle and white muscle. About 10 percent of a shark's muscle is red, which means it has a good blood supply and can work for a long time without tiring. About 90 percent is white muscle, which enables a shark to make short bursts of speed. However, white muscle quickly becomes tired and needs time to recover.

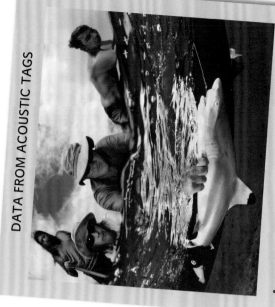

DATA FROM ACOUSTIC TAGS

Acoustic tags fitted to the outside of a shark's body, or inside its abdomen, give off a sound signal that identifies individuals. The signals are picked up by a network of receivers on the seabed. These signals give scientists information about when and where sharks travel, as well as their swimming speed and depths of their dives.

▶ POWERHOUSE
With such powerful muscles, a great white shark can explode right out of the water when hunting its prey. The great white can reach speeds of up to 56 km/h in short bursts.

◀ FLEXIBLE BODIES
Some sharks are so flexible that that they can bend their body right round into a horseshoe shape to completely change direction. Less flexible sharks tilt their front fins and curve their bodies slightly to make more gradual turns.

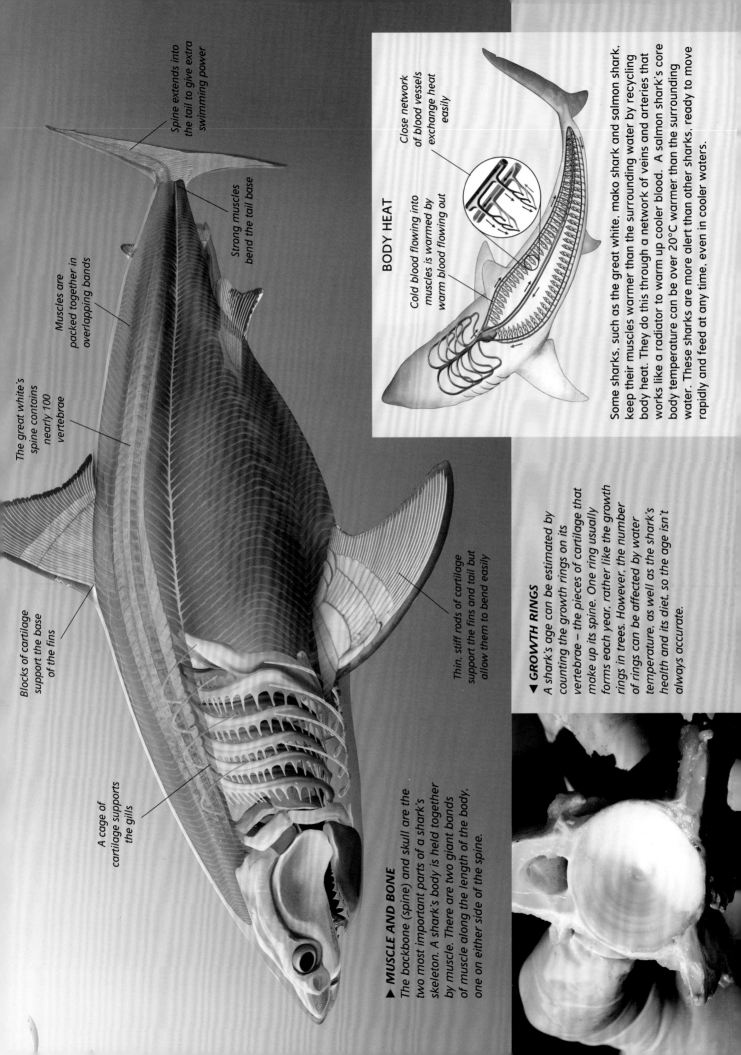

The great white's spine contains nearly 100 vertebrae

Muscles are packed together in overlapping bands

Spine extends into the tail to give extra swimming power

Strong muscles bend the tail base

Blocks of cartilage support the base of the fins

A cage of cartilage supports the gills

Thin, stiff rods of cartilage support the fins and tail but allow them to bend easily

▶ MUSCLE AND BONE

The backbone (spine) and skull are the two most important parts of a shark's skeleton. A shark's body is held together by muscle. There are two giant bands of muscle along the length of the body, one on either side of the spine.

BODY HEAT

Close network of blood vessels exchange heat easily

Cold blood flowing into muscles is warmed by warm blood flowing out

Some sharks, such as the great white, mako shark and salmon shark, keep their muscles warmer than the surrounding water by recycling body heat. They do this through a network of veins and arteries that works like a radiator to warm up cooler blood. A salmon shark's core body temperature can be over 20°C warmer than the surrounding water. These sharks are more alert than other sharks, ready to move rapidly and feed at any time, even in cooler waters.

▶ GROWTH RINGS

A shark's age can be estimated by counting the growth rings on its vertebrae – the pieces of cartilage that make up its spine. One ring usually forms each year, rather like the growth rings in trees. However, the number of rings can be affected by water temperature, as well as the shark's health and its diet, so the age isn't always accurate.

On the move

- **Most sharks** don't have a fixed home. They are constantly swimming, looking for food or a mate.

- **Sharks don't build nests**, dig burrows or make any other kind of shelter.

- **Some species** appear to have a territory, or special area of their own, that they patrol and guard.

- **Whitetip reef sharks** stay in the same area for several months, or even years, although they don't defend it like a true territory.

- **Some sharks**, such as horn sharks, pick a special nursery area in which to lay their eggs.

- **Underwater sea caves** are used by some species as a place to rest during the day.

- **Certain species** of sharks have preferences about where they live. The Galapagos shark is only found around groups of small, tropical oceanic islands.

- **Some sharks** have a daily routine, spending the day in deep waters, but moving to shallow waters near the shore to feed at night.

- **Blacktip reef sharks** seem to prefer their own space. As they swim up and down the edge of a coral reef, individuals will move their jaws or open their mouths to tell other blacktip reef sharks to keep their distance.

- **Some sharks** need to keep moving all the time in order to breathe. These sharks sleep with their eyes open, allowing parts of their brain to rest while they continue swimming.

◄ *Whitetip reef sharks rest during the day on the seabed, and inside underwater caves or rock crevices. At night, they hunt for fish and octopuses among the coral.*

Swimming skills

- **To propel itself** through water, a shark moves its tail from side to side.

- **A shark's fins** help it to balance, to change direction in the water and also to slow down.

- **Sharks normally swim** with a regular rhythm. They don't dart around like most bony fish do.

- **As a shark swims**, its body moves from side to side, forming S-shaped curves.

- **Many species** swim in a figure-of-eight pattern if they feel threatened.

- **Sharks swim silently** through the water and sneak up on prey.

- **Some types**, such as sand tiger sharks, swallow air to help them float better.

- **A shark may use** warm water currents to help it rise higher above the seabed, rather like birds use hot air currents to soar high in the sky.

- **To slow down**, sharks change the angle of their front fins and push against the water. The fins work rather like brakes.

- **A shark's oily liver** helps it to float, because oil is lighter than water. The basking shark's giant liver makes up about one quarter of its body weight and helps it to float at the surface of the sea, where it feeds.

- **Many sharks** don't need to float in the water because they spend a lot of time on the seabed. Some bullhead sharks spend as much time using their fins to 'walk' on the seabed as they do swimming.

▼ *With its slim, streamlined body and long, wing-like front fins, the blue shark is well suited to both cruising near the surface or diving to deeper waters.*

Fast sharks

- **Large sharks** swim at an average speed of about 2.4 km/h, but the most active hunters can speed along much faster when they need to catch prey.

- **It is difficult** for scientists to measure the speed of sharks accurately in the wild because they don't swim in a straight line over a measured course, like a human swimmer.

- **The fastest shark** is the shortfin mako, which can reach speeds of over 50 km/h and possibly over 75 km/h.

- **The mako** has a streamlined body and a pointed snout to cut through the water easily, as well as powerful swimming muscles.

- **The mako needs** to swim fast to catch its speedy prey, such as swordfish and sailfish, which are two of the world's fastest fish.

- **Smaller and chunkier** than its cousin the great white, the salmon shark's top swimming speed rivals that of mako sharks.

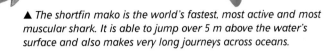

▲ *The shortfin mako is the world's fastest, most active and most muscular shark. It is able to jump over 5 m above the water's surface and also makes very long journeys across oceans.*

- **Salmon sharks** are very acrobatic, often jumping about 6 m above the water as they chase after schools of salmon migrating through the oceans.

- **The blue shark** is like an underwater glider plane, with long front fins and a flat belly. It can reach speeds of up to 40 km/h, gliding down to the ocean depths and then swimming back to the surface again.

- **Compared with a submarine**, a blue shark needs six times less driving power. This is partly due to its rough skin, which reduces the drag of the water by as much as 8 percent.

DID YOU KNOW?

The great white shark can swim seven times faster than the best Olympic swimmers.

Long-distance travel

- **Many shark species** travel long distances over the course of their lives. As all the seas and oceans are connected, it is easy for them to cover huge distances.

- **Dogfish sharks** that have been tagged and released back into the sea have been located more than 8000 km away from where they were first caught.

▼ *This map shows the blue shark's route around the Atlantic Ocean. It travels huge distances after mating to have its pups.*

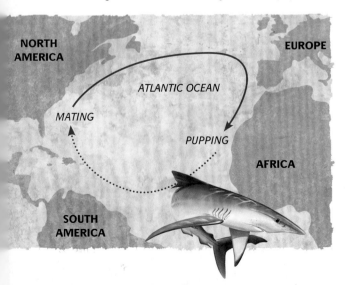

NORTH AMERICA

EUROPE

ATLANTIC OCEAN

MATING

PUPPING

AFRICA

SOUTH AMERICA

- **Migrating means moving around**, usually from season to season, according to a regular pattern.

- **The longest migrations** are made by blue sharks. They swim around the Atlantic Ocean in a huge circle and can cover more than 15,000 km in just one year.

- **Sharks sometimes mate** in one place, then swim far away to another area to lay their eggs or have their pups.

- **They also migrate** to find food, following shoals of fish as they move around the oceans.

- **Scientists think** sharks may use their ampullae of Lorenzini to detect the Earth's magnetic field, helping them to navigate and find their way over long distances.

- **Many species** spend the day in deep water, but swim up to the surface at night. This is called vertical migration.

- **Migrating mako sharks** travel to the middle of the Atlantic Ocean, then turn around and swim back to the USA, where the water is the temperature they prefer to swim in.

Shark fins

- **A typical shark** has up to seven fins, not including its tail.

- **Most sharks** have five different types of fins: dorsal, pectoral, pelvic, anal and caudal (tail) fins. Sharks usually have two dorsal fins, but some species only have one.

- **The large fin** on the back is called the first dorsal fin. It stops a shark's body swinging from side to side while swimming, and sometimes sticks out of the water.

- **Two large pectoral fins** near the front of the body help a shark to steer and stop it from sinking.

- **A shark's two pelvic fins** are beneath its body, by the tail. Like the pectoral fins, they also help to lift the shark up in the water and stop it sinking.

- **A shark has one anal fin**, which is under its body, nearer the tail than the pelvic fins. The anal fin helps to stop the shark from rolling sideways.

- **Megamouth sharks** have soft, rounded fins for swimming slowly in the deep ocean.

- **The wing-like fins** of angelsharks help them to accelerate quickly when they are chasing prey.

- **Epaulette sharks** use their pectoral fins like legs to 'crawl' along the seabed.

- **A whale shark's** pectoral fins are up to 2 m long.

> **DID YOU KNOW?**
>
> Without their fins, sharks wouldn't be able to stay the right way up – they would roll over in the water.

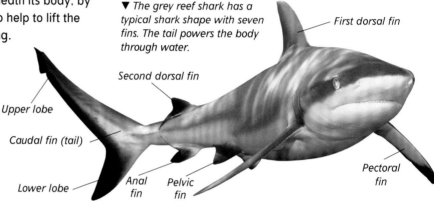

▼ *The grey reef shark has a typical shark shape with seven fins. The tail powers the body through water.*

First dorsal fin

Second dorsal fin

Upper lobe

Caudal fin (tail)

Pectoral fin

Lower lobe

Anal fin

Pelvic fin

Shark tails

- **The tail** is also known as the caudal fin. The anal fin is just in front of the tail.

- **A shark's flattened tail** helps to push it through the water.

- **Sharks that live** at the bottom of the sea, such as the nurse shark, usually have large, flat tails, with a large upper lobe to the tail.

- **Sharks that swim** in the open ocean tend to have slimmer, more curved tails, but still have a larger upper lobe to the tail.

- **The two tail lobes** are an equal size in the fastest sharks, such as the mako shark.

- **This makes** the tail a curved shape and produces a powerful thrust, propelling the shark forwards at high speed.

- **The keel**, or ridge, on the tail of some sharks, such as the porbeagle, mako or great white, provides stability while swimming and probably helps them to turn more easily in the water.

- **Some sharks** smack the surface of the water with their tails to frighten their prey.

- **Thresher sharks** are known for their very long upper tail lobes, which they use to stun prey.

- **Sharks can also** use their tails to sweep across the seabed in order to reveal prey hiding in the sand or mud.

Great white shark

Tiger shark

Bonnethead shark

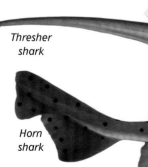

Thresher shark

Horn shark

▶ *The shape of a shark's tail usually indicates its swimming speed. High-speed swimmers (great white shark) have equal upper and lower lobes; cruisers (tiger shark) have a larger upper lobe; slow swimmers (horn shark) have large, flat tails.*

Shark shapes

● **All sharks** have the same basic body plan – a head with eyes, nostrils and a mouth, and a body with a tail and fins.

● **A typical shark** has a long, narrow, torpedo-shaped body. This helps it move quickly through the water.

● **Most sharks** are built for speed and are streamlined in shape. This means water can move past them easily with very little resistance or 'drag'.

● **The tip of a shark's nose** is called the snout. Most are pointed, like the tip of a bullet.

● **Some sharks** have snouts with unusual shapes. Sawsharks have very long, saw-like snouts and the goblin shark has a horn-shaped snout.

● **Frilled sharks** live in the deep sea. Their long, thin bodies are shaped more like those of eels than those of typical sharks.

● **Carpet sharks**, such as wobbegongs, have a flat body shape, which helps them to hide from predators and prey on the seabed.

● **Angelsharks** have wide, spread-out fins that look like wings.

● **Hammerhead sharks** get their name because their heads are shaped like wide, flat hammers.

● **Engineers** sometimes study sharks to determine the best shapes for plane wings or boat hulls.

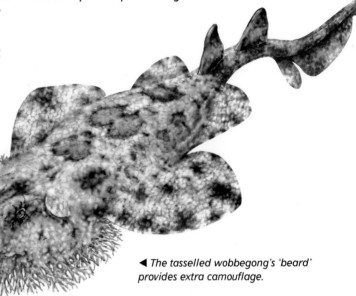

◀ *The tasselled wobbegong's 'beard' provides extra camouflage.*

Sandpaper skin

● **Unlike other fish**, sharks don't have scales. Instead their skin is covered with tiny, hard points called denticles.

● **The word denticle** means 'little tooth'. Denticles range from microscopic in size to about 5 mm across.

● **Denticles** give protection from enemies and help sharks slide easily through the water.

● **If you were to touch** a shark's skin, it would feel very rough. Some swimmers have been badly scratched just from brushing against a shark.

● **The denticles** on the side of a shark's body are the sharpest to ensure fast movement through the water.

● **Many sharks** release a slimy substance from their skin to make their bodies move faster through water.

● **A shark's denticles** overlap like tiles on a roof, which allows the shark's skin to bend.

● **Denticles are very different** from the scales of bony fish, such as salmon. They have the same composition as teeth and are on little stalks.

● **A shark's denticles** eventually fall out and are replaced, just like their teeth.

● **The bramble shark** has large, thorn-like denticles, whereas the silky shark has tiny denticles and a smoother skin than most other sharks.

▼ *A shark's denticles channel the water flowing across its body so as to reduce the energy needed for swimming. They also help sharks to swim quietly, enabling them to sneak up on their prey.*

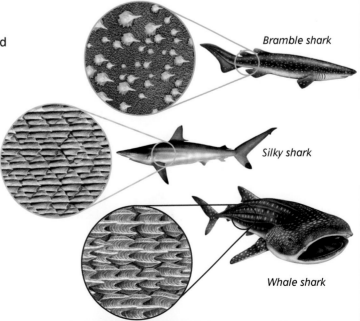

Bramble shark

Silky shark

Whale shark

Staying safe

● **Smaller sharks** make a tasty snack for other animals, so they need to defend themselves against predators, such as dolphins and porpoises.

● **The biggest species** are rarely eaten by other sea creatures, but they can still be hunted by humans.

● **Some sharks** are good at hiding. They slip between rocks or into caves to escape from predators.

● **When in danger**, some species swim in a jerky, random manner to confuse their attacker.

● **Thresher sharks** use their tails to fight off predators, as well as for attacking prey.

● **Shark skin** acts like armour, making it hard for predators to bite them.

● **Species** with spines can often put a predator off by giving it a sharp stab.

● **The sharp spines** of spiny dogfish and Port Jackson sharks inject poison into an attacker.

▶ *A swellshark can puff up its body when it is in a small space in-between rocks. A predator can't pull the shark out because it is wedged in so tightly.*

● **Roughsharks** have large spines on their back but they also have very rough skin, which scratches predators if they try to attack – their skin is rather like barbed wire.

● **Saw sharks** may use their saw-like snouts to defend themselves against predators.

In disguise

● **Many sharks** can disguise themselves to look like their surroundings. This is called camouflage.

● **Camouflage is a good way** to hide from enemies, but it can also be used to help sharks sneak up on their prey without being seen. Many small species, such as zebra sharks, epaulette sharks and wobbegongs, have brown or grey patterns to help them blend in with coral and seaweed.

● **The marbled catshark** is named after the camouflage patterns on its skin, which look like the patterns in marble rock.

▼ *The spots on a young leopard shark's body help to break up its body shape and make it hard to see against a rocky background.*

● **Sharks are often darker** on their top half and paler underneath. This is called countershading. A shark with countershading viewed from below will blend with the brightly lit sea surface. Seen from above, it will blend with the murky depths.

● **Some wobbegong sharks** have barbels that look like seaweed around their mouths. Fish and other prey think the wobbegong is a harmless piece of seaweed and swim right into the shark's open mouth.

● **Angelsharks** have flat, smooth bodies. When they lie on the sandy seabed they become almost invisible.

● **The shovelnose shark** or guitarfish, a type of ray, disguises itself by burying its body in the sand or mud on the sea floor, with only its eyes sticking out.

● **The cookie-cutter shark** uses patches of light on its skin to attract hunting fish, seals or whales to come close – then the cookie-cutter takes a bite out of them.

● **When leopard sharks** are young, they have spots for camouflage. As they get older and bigger, they don't need as much protection, so the spots fade.

A look inside

● **Sharks are vertebrates** – they have a skeleton with a backbone. Many animals, including all fish, reptiles, birds and mammals, are vertebrates.

● **The cartilage** that makes up a shark's skeleton is usually white or pale blue in colour. Because cartilage is flexible, sharks can twist and turn easily in the water.

● **A shark's backbone**, or spine, is made of a string of hourglass-shaped vertebrae under an arch that protects the spinal cord (the main nerve leading from the brain along the spine).

● **A shark's jaws** probably developed from the first arch of cartilage supporting the gills, so are not attached to the shark's skull.

● **Most of the vital organs** are in a cavity in the middle of the body. A shark has many of the same organs as other animals.

● **A shark's heart** pumps blood around its body, delivering oxygen and food nutrients and taking away waste.

● **One-way valves** in each chamber of the heart keep blood flowing in the same direction and prevent it from flowing backwards.

● **The liver** contains lots of oil. Oil is lighter than water, so it helps the shark to float.

● **The stomach** is stretchy. It expands to allow the shark to consume large amounts of food quickly.

● **Sharks have short intestines**, or guts, where nutrients from the shark's food are absorbed into the body.

● **Most sharks** are cold-blooded, which means their blood is the same temperature as the water around them.

● **A shark's brain** controls and co-ordinates its whole body. Networks of nerves carry coded electrical signals to and from the brain.

● **About two thirds** of a shark's brain processes information about smells in the shark's environment.

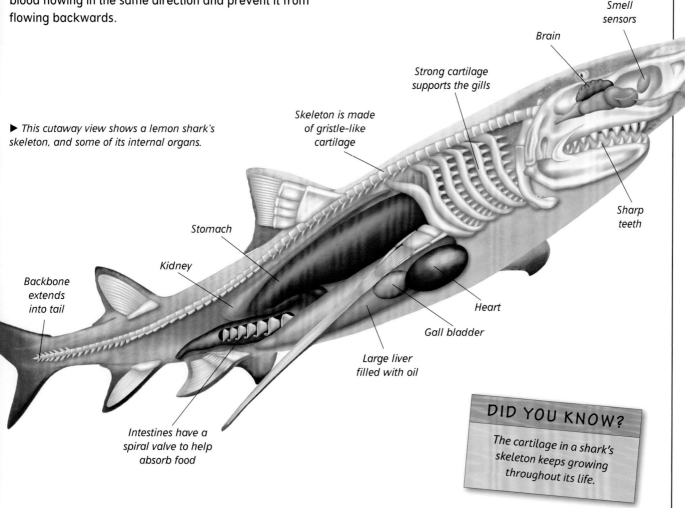

▶ *This cutaway view shows a lemon shark's skeleton, and some of its internal organs.*

Smell sensors

Brain

Strong cartilage supports the gills

Skeleton is made of gristle-like cartilage

Sharp teeth

Stomach

Kidney

Backbone extends into tail

Heart

Gall bladder

Large liver filled with oil

Intestines have a spiral valve to help absorb food

DID YOU KNOW?

The cartilage in a shark's skeleton keeps growing throughout its life.

Gills and breathing

Like all animals, sharks need oxygen to survive. Oxygen helps to convert food into energy, and sharks take in oxygen from the water using their gills. The gills are beneath the slits in the shark's skin on either side of the head. Gills contain tiny blood vessels, which absorb oxygen from the water as it passes over them. Water contains less oxygen than air, so sharks need plenty of water flowing over their gills to allow them to breathe.

Fast-moving sharks have to keep swimming in order to breathe. Water flows into a shark's body through its mouth and out through the gill slits. The gills absorb oxygen from the water and pass it into the blood. They also get rid of carbon dioxide, the waste gas from breathing, by passing it from the blood back into the water.

Slow-moving sharks, or those resting on the seabed, may use muscles to pump water over their gills. Sharks that live on the seafloor often rely on extra breathing holes. These holes, called spiracles, are located on the shark's head, behind its eyes. The shark sucks water into its spiracles and the water flows out through the gill slits. This means that these sharks can breathe even if they are buried in sand and mud, as they don't need to open their mouths to take in water. Rays and skates also do this.

BREATHING WHILE RESTING

To breathe, sharks have to keep water flowing over their gills. When a nurse shark rests on the seabed, it opens its mouth to take in water, but keeps its gill slits closed. Then it closes its mouth, opens its gills and uses the strong muscles in its mouth and neck to push water out over its gills.

▼ GILL RAKERS
A basking shark uses its gills for feeding as well as for breathing. Its huge gill slits go almost right around its head. Slimy bristles called gill rakers, which are in front of the gills, trap small particles of food such as plankton, from the water. A basking shark has more than 5000 gill rakers. To feed, it swims with its mouth wide open.

▲ SPIRACLES
Most sharks, such as this starry smoothhound shark, have five pairs of gill slits. The starry smoothhound shark also has two small breathing holes, or spiracles, which are positioned well behind its eyes.

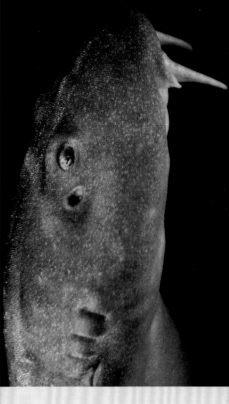

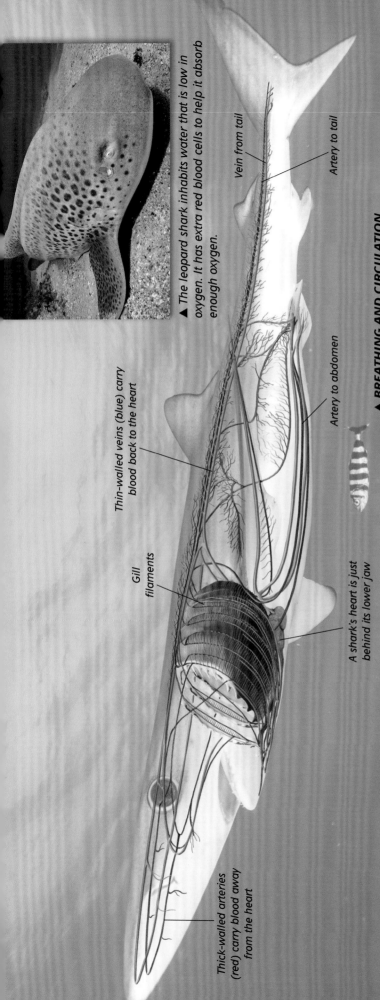

▲ The leopard shark inhabits water that is low in oxygen. It has extra red blood cells to help it absorb enough oxygen.

Vein from tail

Artery to tail

Thin-walled veins (blue) carry blood back to the heart

Gill filaments

Artery to abdomen

A shark's heart is just behind its lower jaw

Thick-walled arteries (red) carry blood away from the heart

▲ **BREATHING AND CIRCULATION**

A shark's gills consist of a set of hair-like filaments full of blood vessels, which is why the gills are red. These blood vessels have very thin walls to allow oxygen to pass quickly from the water into the blood. The blood is pumped around a shark's body by its heart. The blood travels to the gills to pick up oxygen, then flows around the body to deliver the oxygen, before returning to the heart.

▶ **LARGE SPIRACLES**

Blind sharks have large spiracles, which help them to breathe, even when their snouts are buried in the seabed searching for food. These sharks feed on cuttlefish, shellfish, squid, sea anemones and crabs. They are not really blind but are named after their habit of closing their eyes tightly if they are pulled out of the water.

GILL FILAMENTS

Cross section through gills

Plate-like lamellae inside gills to absorb oxygen

Water low in oxygen passes out of the gills

Water filled with oxygen

The filaments in a shark's gills are divided into tiny, leaf-like branches, called lamellae. The lamellae provide a large surface area for absorbing as much oxygen as possible from the water.

Eyes and vision

- **Sharks have well developed eyes**, which work in a range of light levels but sharks probably can't see in colour.

- **Sharks need** to be able to see well in the dark as there is limited light underwater.

- **Some species** have a special eyelid called the nictitating membrane. This closes over the eye when the shark is about to bite, to protect it from damage.

- **White sharks** and whale sharks don't have nictitating membranes. Instead, they swivel their eyes back into their eye sockets to protect them. This means they can't see their prey as they bite.

- **Many sharks** have a layer of shiny plates called the tapetum lucidum (Latin for 'bright carpet') at the back of their eyes. It collects and reflects light, helping them to see, even in the gloomy darkness.

- **The tapetum lucidum** makes shark eyes appear to glow in the dark. In very bright light, the tapetum can be covered with dark coloured cells, which work rather like sunglasses to protect the sensitive layer at the back of the eye.

- **Deepwater and nocturnal** sharks have huge, glowing, green eyes to capture as much light as possible in the darkness.

- **Some sharks** have a third eye, called a pineal eye, under the skin in their foreheads. It can't see as well as a normal eye, but it can sense daylight.

- **The shy-eye shark** gets its name because when it is caught, it covers its eyes with its tail to shield them from the light.

- **A shark's eyes** are ten times more sensitive to light than our eyes. However, sharks can't judge distances as well as we can.

▼ *Some species, such as blacktip reef sharks, have cat-like, slit-shaped pupils.*

Sensing smells

- **As a shark swims**, water constantly flows into the nostrils on its snout. It then travels over the scent-detecting cells inside the nostrils. A shark uses its nostrils purely for detecting scents in the water.

- **The sense of smell** is the most important sense for many sharks.

- **Sharks can smell blood** in water, even if it's diluted to one part in ten million. That's like one pinhead-sized drop of blood in a bathtub of water.

- **Swimmers** have been known to attract sharks just by having a tiny scratch on their skin.

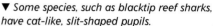

- **Sharks use their sense of smell** to detect prey, but probably also to detect mates and to help them find their way on long migration journeys.

- **Some sharks** can detect smells in the air. Oceanic whitetip sharks sometimes point their noses up through the water's surface to see if there is any smelly food nearby, such as a rotting whale carcass.

- **The biggest parts** of a shark's brain are the olfactory lobes – the area used for processing smells.

- **The great white** has the biggest olfactory lobes of all sharks, which means it probably has the best sense of smell.

- **A shark homes in** on a scent by zigzagging its snout from side to side and then moving towards the side where the smell is strongest.

◄ *The nostrils of hammerhead sharks are at the tips of their 'hammers', so they smell in stereo, which helps these sharks to track down the source of a smell.*

Touch and taste

● **Like us**, sharks can feel things that touch their skin. They have millions of nerve endings that can feel pressure, temperature and pain.

● **They also have** an extra sense organ called the lateral line. This is a long tube running down each side of a shark's body, under its skin. All fish, not just sharks, have lateral lines.

● **As a shark swims**, ripples in the water pass into the lateral line through tiny holes in the skin. Hairs inside sense the ripples, and send signals to the brain.

● **The shark's brain** interprets the signals from its lateral line as possible prey, predators or other sharks.

● **The lateral line** also helps a shark to keep its balance and avoid bumping into objects in its surroundings.

▶ *The lateral line runs down the side of the entire length of a shark's body.*

● **As it is most effective** for picking up vibrations close to the shark's body, the lateral line helps sharks to find their way in murky or dark water, when their other senses are not much use.

● **Sharks taste the animals** or objects they bite with the tastebuds inside their mouths. They can also taste chemicals dissolved in the water. This helps them to find prey and avoid pollution.

● **Sharks use** their sense of taste to help them decide whether to swallow or spit out an object or piece of food. Great white sharks tend to spit out human flesh. They prefer the taste of fatty blubber from their usual prey, such as seals.

● **Some species** have fleshy whiskers on their snouts called barbels, which help them to sense the location of food on the seabed.

● **Sharks with barbels** include nurse sharks, bamboo sharks, sawsharks and wobbegongs.

Hearing sounds

● **Sharks have ears**, but they're hard to spot. The openings are tiny holes, just behind the eyes. People sometimes mistake the spiracles, which are used for breathing, for ears.

● **In the sea**, sound travels in the form of vibrations rippling through the water. Sharks hear by sensing these vibrations.

● **Inside the ear** is a set of looping, fluid-filled tubes called the labyrinth. Inside the labyrinth are microscopic hairs. Vibrations travel through the fluid, moving the hairs, which send signals to the shark's brain.

● **Sharks hear** low sounds best, such as the noise made by an injured animal underwater.

● **Sharks can pick up** these sounds from around 200 m away.

● **Ears also help sharks** to keep their balance. The movement of fluid inside their ears tells them which way up they are.

● **The grey reef shark** has a very well-developed balance system in its inner ear. This helps it to keep its balance when swimming in a large group of reef sharks.

● **The sound of research submersibles** can easily be detected by sharks and may frighten deep-sea sharks, making it difficult for scientists to study them.

● **Sharks gather** at popular shark feeding sites when they hear the sounds of boat engines, which they learn to associate with food.

▲ *Sharks can also detect the sounds of air bubbles coming from scuba-diving tanks, so this blue shark can hear the diver breathing.*

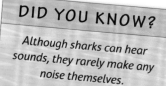

The sixth sense

- **A shark has six senses**. Besides vision, hearing, touch, taste and smell, it can sense the tiny amounts of electricity given off by other animals.

- **To detect electricity**, a shark has tiny holes in the skin around its head and snout. They are called the ampullae of Lorenzini.

- **The ampullae of Lorenzini** are named after Stefano Lorenzini (born c.1652). He was an Italian scientist who studied the anatomy of sharks.

- **Ampullae** are a type of Roman bottle. The ampullae of Lorenzini have a narrow-necked bottle shape.

- **Each ampulla** contains a jelly-like substance, which collects electrical signals.

- **All animals** give off tiny amounts of electricity when their muscles move. Electricity doesn't travel well through air, but it does through water.

DID YOU KNOW?

Some other animals, such as the duck-billed platypus, can detect electricity too.

- **The ampullae of Lorenzini** can sense animals within a range of about one metre.

- **Some sharks** use their electrical sense to find prey that is buried in the seabed.

- **A fierce hunting species**, such as the tiger shark, has up to 1500 ampullae of Lorenzini.

- **Slow-moving sharks** that live on the seabed have only a few hundred ampullae of Lorenzini.

- **Sharks sometimes bite** on seabed cables because these objects produce electric signals.

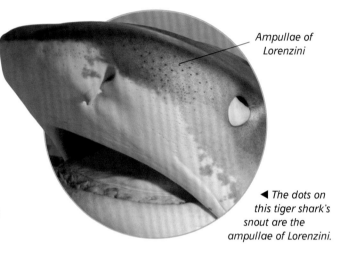

Ampullae of Lorenzini

◀ The dots on this tiger shark's snout are the ampullae of Lorenzini.

Smart sharks

- **Most shark species** have big brains for their body size and are probably smarter than many bony fish.

- **Almost all of the brain** is used for processing information from the senses. The parts used for learning and thinking are small.

- **In relation to their body size**, hammerhead sharks have the biggest brains.

◀ A scientist releasing a young lemon shark during a study of how lemon sharks avoid predators in the wild. Studying the behaviour of young sharks helps scientists to understand more about how sharks learn to survive.

- **Scalloped hammerheads** are one of the smartest sharks. They are fast, fierce hunters.

DID YOU KNOW?

Captive lemon sharks learn how to perform scientific tests 80 times faster than cats or rabbits.

- **Hammerheads** spend time in groups and scientists think they have simple social systems.

- **In captivity**, some sharks have learned to do simple tasks in exchange for rewards.

- **Captive lemon sharks** have been taught to ring bells, press targets, swim through mazes and recover rings in order to receive rewards of food.

- **Sharks are curious** and inquisitive animals. They are able to solve problems, as well as to learn and remember things. All these qualities are signs of intelligence.

- **Some species** are brighter than others. Fast hunters such as great whites are the most intelligent. Slow-moving bottom-feeders such as carpet sharks are less smart.

Food and feeding

● **Large, fast, hunting sharks**, such as great whites and bull sharks, feed on large fish (including other sharks), as well as seals, turtles, octopuses, squid, seabirds and other sea creatures.

● **Smaller sharks**, such as dogfish sharks, hunt smaller fish, octopuses and squid.

● **Slow-moving species**, such as nurse sharks, angelsharks and carpet sharks, crunch up crabs, shrimps and shellfish that they find on the seabed.

● **Filter-feeders** feed on plankton – tiny floating animals and plants – which they filter from the water.

● **There are hardly** any animal species in the sea that aren't part of the diet of one shark species or another.

● **Tiger sharks** will eat anything they can find, even objects that aren't food, such as tin cans.

● **Most sharks** don't eat every day. Some large hunters can go without food for months.

● **Some sharks prefer** to eat just a few types of food. Giant hammerhead sharks like to eat stingrays and the sicklefin weasel shark prefers a diet of octopus.

● **Big sharks** often feed on smaller sharks. Some sharks are cannibals, eating sharks of their own species. Tiger sharks are cannibals.

● **A big shark** can eat more than half its own body weight in one meal.

▼ *When small fish are in danger from sharks, they often cluster together in a tight sphere called a bait ball. These bronze whaler sharks have disturbed the cluster to make the fish easier to catch.*

Teeth and jaws

● **A hunting species**, such as the great white or the tiger shark, has several rows of teeth.

● **Only the two front rows** of teeth are used for biting. The rest are lining up to replace them when they wear out or break.

● **In a lifetime**, some sharks will get through 30,000 teeth. You can sometimes find shark teeth washed up on beaches.

● **Some shark teeth**, such as those of bull sharks, have serrated edges (like a saw) and are as sharp as razors. This allows them to slice through meat easily.

● **The biggest teeth** belong to the great white shark. Its teeth can grow to more than 6 cm in length.

● **Some species**, such as smooth-hound sharks, don't have sharp biting teeth. Instead they have hard, flat plates in their mouths for grinding up crabs and shellfish.

● **The outside of a shark's teeth** is made up of fluoride – an ingredient in most toothpastes as it prevents tooth decay. This means that sharks don't get holes in their teeth.

◀ *The tiger shark has large, saw-edged, hooked teeth in both jaws. It has a varied diet, from fish, sea snakes, sea turtles and seabirds, to jellyfish, rotting meat and rubbish.*

▶ *Port Jackson sharks have small, sharp, pointed teeth at the front of their jaws and large flattened teeth at the back, for crushing sea urchins, starfish and shellfish.*

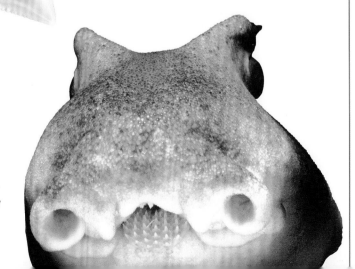

Going hunting

● **Most sharks are nocturnal** – they hunt at night – or crepuscular – they hunt at dusk.

● **Sharks use several senses** to track down and home in on prey. They locate it from a distance by smell, and use their electric sense, sight and hearing to close in on it. Sharks can also feel ripples in the water made by the movement of other animals.

● **Before attacking**, some sharks 'bump' their prey with their snouts, probably to see if it's edible.

● **When it is about to bite**, a shark raises its snout and thrusts its jaws forwards, so that its teeth stick out.

● **Sometimes lots of sharks** are attracted to a source of food, and they all rush to eat it at the same time. This is known as a feeding frenzy.

● **Most hunters** prefer prey that's weak or helpless because it's easier to catch. Sharks are good at smelling blood – it tells them when an animal is injured.

● **Many species** give their prey a fatal bite, then move away while it bleeds to death. They return later to feed on the body.

● **A great white shark** usually attacks from behind or below so its prey does not see it coming. It moves so fast, it may leap right out of the water with its victim in its jaws.

● **Some sharks**, such as whitetip reef sharks, silky sharks and spiny dogfish work together to catch prey. They catch more food by working as a team.

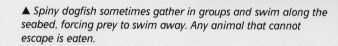

▲ *Spiny dogfish sometimes gather in groups and swim along the seabed, forcing prey to swim away. Any animal that cannot escape is eaten.*

● **Tiny pygmy sharks** hunt together so they can catch and kill fish much bigger than themselves.

● **Blacktip reef sharks** co-operate to drive fish into shallow water and onto the beach. Then they wriggle onto the beach, grab the fish and slide back into the sea.

● **A group of sharks**, such as silky sharks or sandtiger sharks, will often herd fish into a tight ball by swimming towards them from different directions. The sharks then grab the fish swimming on the outside of the ball.

● **When many young seabirds** or seals enter the water for the first time, groups of sharks, such as tiger sharks, gather to eat as much as they can.

◄ *A school of lemon sharks stirs up clouds of white sand as individuals compete for their share of food.*

DID YOU KNOW?

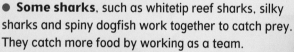

Sharks have very strong jaws. Some can bite other animals in half – even those with tough shells, such as turtles.

Filter feeding

- **The biggest shark species** of all – whale sharks, basking sharks and megamouths – eat plankton, which is the smallest prey. These sharks are called filter-feeders.

- **Plankton** is made up of small sea creatures such as shrimps, baby crabs and squid, little fish and tiny, free-floating plants. It drifts along with the currents.

- **Filter-feeding sharks** have gill rakers. These are comb-like bristles in their throats that sieve plankton out of the water.

- **Gill rakers are coated** in mucus to help plankton stick to them.

- **Filter-feeders swallow** the plankton they have collected, while water they have sieved escapes from their gills.

- **These sharks have massive mouths**, so they can suck in as much water as possible.

- **To collect a kilogram of plankton**, a shark has to filter one million litres of water.

- **In one hour**, a whale shark filters around 2 million litres of water, and collects 2 kg of food.

▲ *Whale sharks open their big mouths wide to take in lots of water. Then they filter plankton from the water as it flows over their comb-like gills and back out of the body.*

- **Whale sharks** sometimes suck in shoals of little fish, such as sardines, that are also busy feeding on plankton.

- **The blue whale**, the world's biggest animal, is also a filter-feeder.

Scavenging food

- **Scavenging** means feeding on other hunters' leftovers, or on animals that are dying or already dead.

- **Almost all sharks** will scavenge if they cannot find other food.

- **Some species**, such as the Greenland shark and the smooth dogfish, get a lot of their food by scavenging.

- **In deep water**, sharks often feed on dead sea creatures that sink down from higher levels.

- **Sharks scavenge** human food too, especially waste food that's thrown overboard from ships.

- **Sometimes sharks eat fish** caught in fishing nets before the nets are pulled to the surface.

- **Great whites** also scavenge, especially on the bodies of dead whales.

- **Scavenging is natural recycling**. It cleans the oceans, and ensures leftovers and dead animals are rapidly removed rather than left to slowly decompose.

- **The tiger shark** is famous for its scavenging habits and will eat almost any dead meat, from fish, squid and sea snakes to seals, dolphins and whales.

- **Tiger sharks** will also eat the carcasses of land animals, such as chickens, dogs, horses and cows that are washed into the sea.

▼ *It can take up to 100 years for a whale carcass to be eaten by scavengers. More than 30,000 different types of animal feed and live off the carcass at different stages.*

DID YOU KNOW?

Old, rotting meat is bad for humans to eat, but many wild animals such as sharks can eat it safely.

Teeth and digestion

Most sharks use their teeth for catching and killing prey. They don't usually chew their food. Instead, prey is torn into chunks, or swallowed whole. Some sharks even shake prey from side to side to rip it apart. So the process of breaking down, or digesting, food does not start until it enters the shark's digestive system. Digesting a meal can take up to four hours.

A shark's digestive system consists of a long tube, with an entry point (the mouth) at one end and an exit hole (the cloaca) at the other end. Food that cannot be digested leaves the shark's body through the cloaca, which is between its pelvic fins, near the tail.

When a shark swallows food, it slides down into its stomach. The muscular walls of the stomach churn up the food and strong digestive juices and acids break the food down into a soupy paste. A shark's stomach is like a stretchy bag, which can hold large meals. From the stomach, the partly digested food passes into the shark's intestine. Muscular waves in the walls of the intestine move the food along. Further digestive juices then break the food down, and nutrients are absorbed through the walls of the intestine.

STOMACH CLEANSING

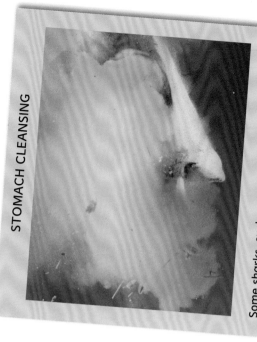

Some sharks, such as lemon, tiger and mako sharks, can project their stomach right out of the mouth to get rid of indigestible items they have swallowed. In just a few seconds, they push their stomach out into the water, shake it to rinse it clean and swallow it back into place again.

▼ SPINNER SHARK
Spinner sharks spin right out of the water when hunting schools of fish. They turn round and round up to three times before falling back into the water.

▲ SCAVENGING
The tiger shark eats the bodies of dead animals, such as this whale. It is attracted by the smell of rotting meat in the water. This food is already partly broken down by bacteria and other sea creatures, so it doesn't take the shark as long to digest as a freshly caught meal.

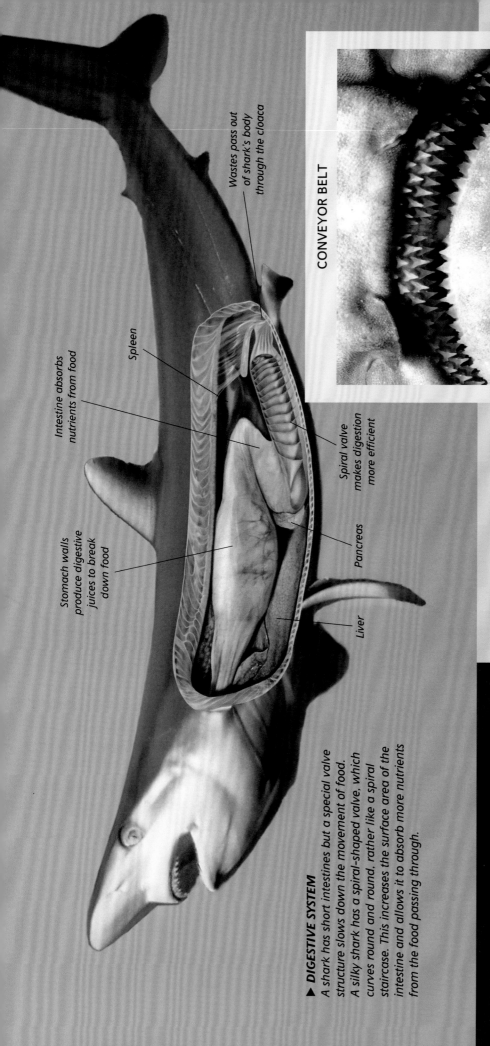

► DIGESTIVE SYSTEM

A shark has short intestines but a special valve structure slows down the movement of food. A silky shark has a spiral-shaped valve, which curves round and round, rather like a spiral staircase. This increases the surface area of the intestine and allows it to absorb more nutrients from the food passing through.

Stomach walls produce digestive juices to break down food

Intestine absorbs nutrients from food

Spleen

Spiral valve makes digestion more efficient

Pancreas

Liver

Wastes pass out of shark's body through the cloaca

CONVEYOR BELT

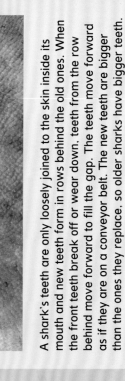

A shark's teeth are only loosely joined to the skin inside its mouth and new teeth form in rows behind the old ones. When the front teeth break off or wear down, teeth from the row behind move forward to fill the gap. The teeth move forward as if they are on a conveyor belt. The new teeth are bigger than the ones they replace, so older sharks have bigger teeth.

▼ VARIOUS VALVES

A shark has one of three main valve shapes inside its intestines: a spiral valve (1), a scroll valve (2), or a ring valve (3). Ring valves have many thin plates packed tightly together – a great white shark has a ring valve in its intestine. Scroll valves are made up of one long, thin fold of skin, like a loose scroll of paper. Lemon sharks and hammerhead sharks have scroll valves inside their intestines.

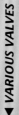

Loners and groups

● **Many shark species**, such as bull sharks, are solitary. This means that they live alone.

● **Sharks don't live** in families. They meet up to mate, but do not stay together afterwards. Once born, young sharks do not live with their parents either.

● **Some sharks form groups** with other members of their species. Whitetip reef sharks often rest together in small groups of about ten individuals.

▼ *During the day, hammerhead sharks hunt together in schools. At night, they separate to hunt alone.*

● **Sharks may form** groups because there is safety in numbers. A group is less likely to be attacked than a single shark.

● **Being in a group** may also help sharks to find a mate.

● **Some species**, such as lemon sharks, blue sharks and spiny dogfish, form single-sex groups of just males or females outside the breeding season. Scientists are not sure why.

● **Basking sharks** have been seen in groups of 50 or more, in places where there is lots of plankton floating on the sea for them to eat.

● **Great white sharks** sometimes travel in pairs or small groups.

● **Two or three great white sharks** may sometimes hunt together and share each other's meals.

● **Shark pups** often stay together in shallow water 'nurseries', well away from larger adult sharks, which might eat them.

Sending messages

● **Animals don't have** complicated languages like humans – but they can still communicate.

● **Sharks can 'talk'** using body language. They make different postures, just as humans show their feelings using different expressions.

● **When a shark is aggressive** or frightened, it arches its back, raises its snout, and points its pectoral fins down.

● **Sharks also release** special scents called pheromones to send messages to other sharks. These can indicate if a shark is looking for a mate or feeling agitated.

● **When they live in a group**, the strongest sharks usually become the leaders. They will sometimes fight with the other sharks to show their dominance.

● **A few species** can make sounds. Swellsharks can make a barking noise, but experts are not sure if it is a way of communicating.

● **A threatened sand tiger shark** makes a sound rather like a gunshot when it slaps its tail loudly on the water's surface.

● **Great white sharks** warn rivals to keep away by showing their sharp teeth, splashing their tail at the surface, or even hitting a rival with their strong tail.

● **If a rival does not back off**, the great white will give it a small bite and hope that it swims away without the need for a fight, which may injure both sharks.

● **Part of the threat display** of the grey reef shark is to swim stiffly in a figure-of-eight loop.

▲ *This shark is displaying aggression. Its raised snout, arched back and lowered fins mean it is ready to attack.*

Meeting and mating

● **Like most animals**, sharks have to mate in order to reproduce and have offspring (babies).

● **During mating**, a male and female shark of the same species join together. Sperm cells from the male fertilize the egg cells inside the female to begin the development of a new shark.

● **Sometimes females** store sperm from a male shark for fertilization in the future, perhaps in a year or more.

● **When they mate**, the male shark uses his claspers to place sperm into an opening in the female's body, called the cloaca.

● **A small, flexible male shark**, such as a dogfish, wraps its body tightly around the female to get in the right position for mating.

● **Larger sharks**, such as whitetip reef sharks, with more rigid bodies, mate swimming side by side or with their heads down and their undersides together.

● **Shark mating usually takes** from 15 to 30 minutes and then the pair go their separate ways.

● **Many species**, including nurse sharks and blue sharks, have special mating areas in shallow parts of the sea.

● **In other species**, such as whitetip reef sharks, females release chemicals called pheromones to help males locate them.

● **Males sometimes bite** females to show that they want to mate with them.

● **Females often have thicker skin** than males (up to three times as thick) so that being bitten during courtship doesn't harm them.

● **Sharks don't mate very often**. Most species only reproduce once every two years.

● **Lemon sharks** mate while slowly swimming along, with the back of their bodies touching, but their heads apart.

▶ *Male whitetip reef sharks sometimes spend time resting in shallow water during the day. If they smell a pheromone scent from a female, they will try to find her.*

Male and female sharks

● **In most species of sharks**, the females are larger than the males. This may help them to produce large eggs, or look after the developing pups inside their bodies.

● **Female sharks** may weigh up to a quarter more than male sharks of the same species.

● **Male and female sharks** look similar on the outside. The main difference is that males have two claspers for delivering sperm to the females.

● **The claspers** of a male shark are folds of skin with grooves. They are formed from the inner sides of the pelvic fins, which are rolled around like a scroll.

● **Each clasper** has a mechanism for pumping the sperm through the channel in the middle of the scroll.

● **Claspers vary** in different species. They may be flat, round, smooth or covered with denticles (skin scales) shaped like hooks or spurs.

● **Inside a female shark** there are usually two ovaries, which make eggs, and two egg tubes, called oviducts.

● **Sperm from a male shark** fertilizes the eggs inside the oviducts of the female shark.

● **After fertilization**, the eggs are covered with a tough, protective covering and move into the female's womb, or uterus, which has two chambers.

Male

Female

◄ *Male blacktip reef sharks are smaller than females. Males are 91–100 cm long, whereas females are 96–112 cm long.*

Laying eggs

● **Many sharks** have young by laying eggs. Most bony fish also reproduce this way.

● **Sharks that lay eggs** are called oviparous sharks. They typically lay between ten and 20 eggs at a time.

● **About 40 percent** of sharks lay eggs that hatch outside the female's body.

▼ *A baby catshark develops slowly in its protective case. At 50 days it is smaller than the yolk, its store of food.*

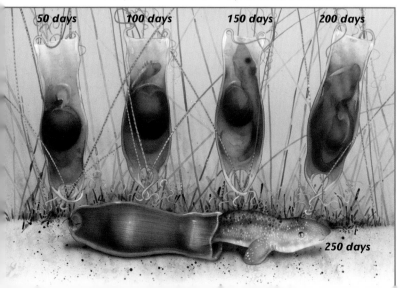

50 days   100 days   150 days   200 days

250 days

● **Oviparous species** include bullhead sharks, dogfish sharks, horn sharks, zebra sharks, swellsharks, bamboo sharks, wobbegong sharks and many catsharks.

DID YOU KNOW?

Female skates and chimaeras also lay eggs with leathery egg cases to protect their developing young.

● **A mother shark** doesn't guard her eggs. She lays them in a safe place, such as between two rocks or under a clump of seaweed, then leaves them to hatch.

● **The eggs are enclosed** in cases, which allow oxygen to pass in and body wastes to pass out.

● **Inside the egg**, the baby shark grows for between six and 12 months before hatching.

● **When the baby shark** hatches out of the egg, it looks like its parents.

● **Female sharks** lay relatively large eggs compared to their body size. For instance, a female shark about 1.8 m long lays egg cases 5–10 cm long.

● **A huge female whale shark** lays eggs cases up to 30 cm long.

Giving birth

- **Not all sharks lay eggs.** Some give birth to live young. These sharks are known as viviparous or ovoviviparous.

- **In ovoviviparous species**, such as basking sharks, the young, called pups, grow inside eggs. They hatch out while inside the mother's body, before being born.

- **About 40 percent** of all sharks are ovoviviparous, including frilled sharks, sand sharks, thresher sharks, tiger sharks, nurse sharks and mako sharks.

- **In viviparous sharks**, such as hammerheads, the pups grow inside the mother's body, but not in eggs.

- **Viviparous sharks** develop inside the mother's uterus, or womb, where they receive food through a structure called a placenta, which develops from the pup's yolk sac. The placenta is attached to the wall of the mother's uterus.

- **Mother sharks** with pups developing inside them like this are 'pregnant'. Most shark pregnancies last up to about one year.

- **Some shark pregnancies** are much longer. In the spiny dogfish, pregnancy lasts up to two years.

▲ A newborn lemon shark swims away from its mother. Lemon shark pups are 60–65 cm long at birth.

- **In sand tiger sharks** and several other species, the strongest pups eat the others while they are still inside the mother's body.

- **Baby hammerhead sharks** are born head-first, but have their 'hammer-heads' folded back to avoid harming their mother.

Newborn sharks

- **Most shark pups** look like smaller versions of their parents. They often have a narrower body shape and stronger colours.

- **Some species**, such as sand tiger sharks, give birth to just two pups in a single litter.

- **The pups of some species** are born with the yolk still attached. The yolk continues to nourish the shark as it grows.

- **The long, thin shape** of newborn sharks makes them look more like water snakes, which means that predators are less likely to attack them.

- **Mako sharks** produce large, strong pups, which are ready to swim in the open ocean and begin hunting as soon as they are born.

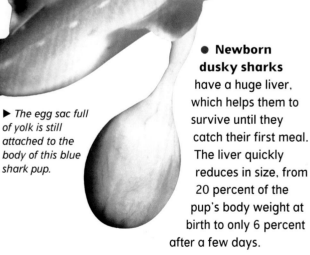

▶ The egg sac full of yolk is still attached to the body of this blue shark pup.

- **Newborn dusky sharks** have a huge liver, which helps them to survive until they catch their first meal. The liver quickly reduces in size, from 20 percent of the pup's body weight at birth to only 6 percent after a few days.

- **Lemon sharks** hide among seaweed in shallow water for the first two years after they are born, before moving to deeper water.

- **Blue sharks** give birth to up to 135 pups at a time. The pups are about 51 cm long when they are born.

- **Some female sharks**, such as bonnethead sharks, zebra sharks, blacktip sharks and whitespotted bamboo sharks, are able to give birth to pups without mating with a male shark.

Growing up

- **Many sharks** grow rather slowly and mature late in life. It can take a shark pup 10–20 years or more to mature into an adult.

- **This makes it difficult** for sharks to adapt quickly to new environmental conditions or to keep up their numbers when so many of them are killed by people.

- **Blue sharks** are among the fastest-growing. A pup grows about 20 cm every year.

- **A Greenland shark** grows very slowly, only increasing in size by about 0.5 cm a year.

- **Greenland sharks** could live to be more than 300 years old.

- **As pups are small**, they are good targets for predators. The biggest danger comes from adult sharks. Pups may even be eaten by adults of their own species.

- **For every ten pups born**, only one or two will survive to be adults.

- **Many species** of pups live in 'nursery areas' – shallow parts of the sea close to the shore, where there are plenty of places to hide and smaller sea creatures to hunt.

- **Sharks are born** with a full set of teeth, so they can start to hunt straight away.

▲ *Small lemon sharks are often eaten by larger sharks. This is why they spend the first few years of their lives living along sheltered shorelines, such as this mangrove swamp.*

- **Adult sharks** don't look after their babies. Once the pup is born, or has hatched, it has to fend for itself.

- **A typical shark** lives for around 25–30 years, although some species, such as whale sharks and dogfish sharks, may live for 100 years or more.

- **Great white sharks** could live to be at least 73 years old.

- **Sharks keep growing** all through their lives, although they grow more slowly as they become older.

- **Sharks also grow** more slowly in cold conditions and when food is hard to find.

- **Blue sharks** and mako sharks grow much faster than Greenland sharks when food is plentiful. They may grow up to 20 cm or more per year.

DID YOU KNOW?

Male great white sharks are about 26 years old before they are ready to mate; female great whites aren't ready to have babies until they are about 33 years old.

Friends and enemies

▲ *These remora fish feed on scraps and parasites from this lemon shark, as well as gaining protection from predators.*

● **There are several types** of sea creature that have a close relationship with sharks. These include some fish species and parasites that feed on the skin, blood or insides of sharks.

● **Small, crab-like creatures** called copepods attach themselves to a shark's eyes, gills, snout or fins. They nibble the shark's skin or suck its blood.

● **Copepods on the eyes** of Greenland sharks damage the surface of the eyes and make it more difficult for these sharks to see clearly. Sea leeches bite sharks on their undersides and suck their blood.

● **Many shark species** have tapeworms inside their guts. They feed on the shark's food.

● **Whale sharks** sometimes try to get rid of skin parasites, such as barnacles, by rubbing up against boats. The barnacles make the shark swim more slowly and may provide a route for an infection to get under the shark's skin.

● **Sometimes two species** can help each other. This kind of relationship between two animals is called symbiosis, which means 'living together'.

● **Many sharks** visit 'cleaning stations' where small fish and shrimps remove dead skin and parasites from their bodies – even from inside their mouth or gills.

● **Basking sharks** are sometimes covered with sea lamprey fish, which use their suckers to grip tightly to the shark's skin. These sharks may sometimes leap out of the water and crash back down again to try and dislodge the lampreys.

● **Remoras or 'shark suckers'** are fish that attach themselves to sharks using suction pads on their heads. They hitch a ride on the shark's body and feed on leftover scraps of food.

● **Sharks open their mouths** to let tiny cleaner wrasse fish nibble lice and dead skin from between their teeth.

● **Small pilotfish** often swim alongside sharks, saving energy by keeping close to the bigger animal, which creates a sheltered 'pathway' through the water. The pilotfish is also protected by the bulk of the shark and able to eat leftover food scraps.

▼ *A Greenland shark with a parasitic copepod attached to its eye.*

STRIPES AND SPOTS

Zebra sharks have striped patterns when they hatch out of their egg cases. As they become adults, the stripes separate into spots. This means that both adults and young are camouflaged from predators. The stripes of the young and the way they swim help to make them look like poisonous banded sea snakes, giving them extra protection.

Eggs and babies

Most sharks give birth to pups after pregnancies lasting from three months in some species to as long as two years or more in others. The number of pups born at any one time also varies with the species of shark, from two pups at once to hundreds of babies for the whale shark. Some sharks, such as dogfish and swellsharks, lay eggs, which are protected inside strong cases.

Shark egg cases come in many shapes, such as tubes, spirals and pillows. Many of them are rather like purses or pouches, with the eggs safely hidden inside. Female sharks lay their eggs in places where there is a good supply of food for the baby sharks. They may take hours to push the egg cases out of their bodies. The cases are soft and flexible at first, but they harden when they come into contact with the seawater. Sharks don't look after their egg cases and many baby sharks do not survive long enough to hatch out. The eggs may be eaten by predators, such as sea snails, or the egg cases may be washed up on beaches, where they dry out so the baby sharks inside them die.

▼ *SPIRAL EGG CASE*
Female Port Jackson sharks lay spiral-shaped egg cases, which they wedge firmly into cracks in rocks. One female lays 10–16 egg cases every eight to 17 days.

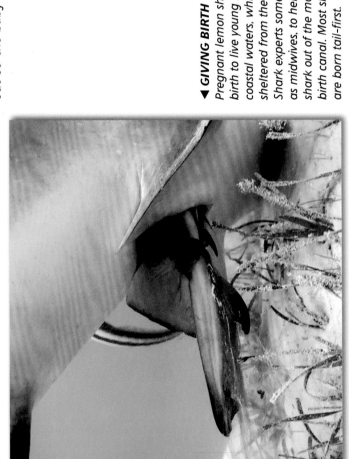

▼ *GIVING BIRTH*
Pregnant lemon sharks give birth to live young in shallow coastal waters, which are sheltered from the waves. Shark experts sometimes act as midwives, to help the baby shark out of the mother's birth canal. Most shark pups are born tail-first.

While inside its egg case, a baby shark gets food from a large yolk sac that is joined to its belly by a cord. Oxygen in the surrounding water passes through the egg case so that the shark can breathe. As it develops, the baby sprouts fins and begins to wriggle about. This shark is about three months into its development.

Eye of baby shark

Long tail of baby shark at 3 months old

Large yolk sac full of nutrients

Cord joins yolk sac to baby shark's body

MERMAID'S PURSE

Empty shark egg cases are sometimes washed up on beaches. Before people understood what these were, they were nicknamed 'mermaids' purses' because they looked as if they could be purses belonging to mythical mermaids.

▼ KEEPING SAFE

Newborn sharks, such as these blacktip reef sharks, are small and slim – usually only about 20–30 cm long. Their small size makes them vulnerable to predators, including adult sharks. They rely on camouflage colours and instinct for self-defence in order to survive.

Types of shark

- **There are more than 500 species** of shark and scientists divide them into eight large groups, called orders. They are then divided into about 34 smaller groups, or families.

- **Arranging species** into groups, or classifying them, helps scientists to study and identify them.

- **Scientists often disagree** about how to classify sharks, so there are several different ways to do it.

- **Shark orders** and families have long scientific names. For example, goblin sharks belong to the Mitsukurinidae family, in the Lamniformes order.

- **Some groups** have common names too. For example, species in the Lamniformes order are also known as mackerel sharks.

- **Each species** has its own scientific name, which is written in Latin. The first part identifies the genus to which the species belongs. The second part identifies the species within the genus.

- **Scientists decide** which group a shark belongs to by looking at features such as its body shape, markings, behaviour and DNA.

- **Sometimes**, very different-looking sharks can belong to the same group. Huge whale sharks and small, slender epaulette sharks are both in the same order.

▶ This diagram shows how different types of shark are thought to be related and the key characteristics of each group.

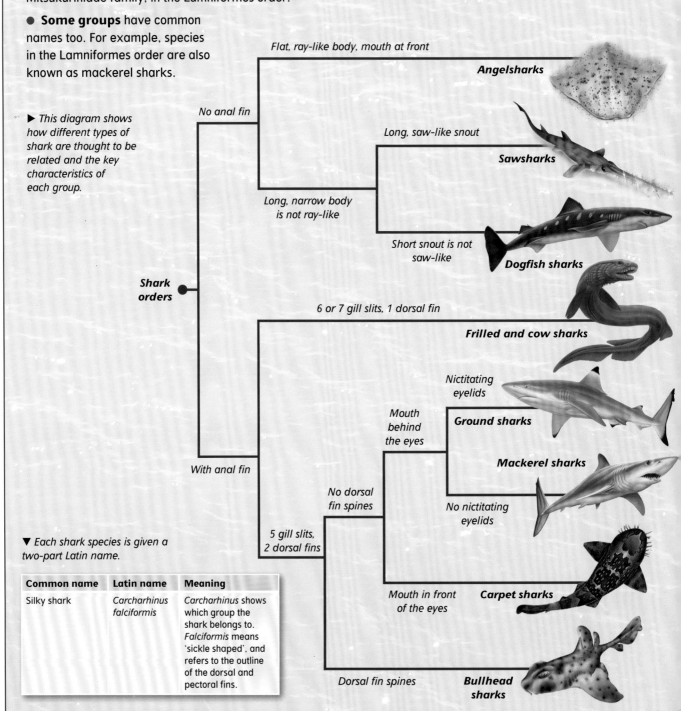

Flat, ray-like body, mouth at front

Angelsharks

No anal fin

Long, saw-like snout

Sawsharks

Long, narrow body is not ray-like

Short snout is not saw-like

Dogfish sharks

Shark orders

6 or 7 gill slits, 1 dorsal fin

Frilled and cow sharks

Nictitating eyelids

Mouth behind the eyes

Ground sharks

Mackerel sharks

With anal fin

No dorsal fin spines

No nictitating eyelids

5 gill slits, 2 dorsal fins

Mouth in front of the eyes

Carpet sharks

Dorsal fin spines

Bullhead sharks

▼ Each shark species is given a two-part Latin name.

Common name	Latin name	Meaning
Silky shark	Carcharhinus falciformis	Carcharhinus shows which group the shark belongs to. Falciformis means 'sickle shaped', and refers to the outline of the dorsal and pectoral fins.

Angelsharks

- **Angelsharks are named** after the wide, wing-like shape of their fins. There are at least 20 species of angelsharks.

- **Monkfish** is another name for angelsharks. People used to think their fins looked like a monk's robes.

- **Like wobbegongs** and other bottom-dwelling sharks, angelsharks are camouflaged with spotted, speckled skin patterns.

- **The ocellated angelshark** has 'eye spots' on its side fins and the base of the tail. These may help to divert attention away from the shark's real eyes.

- **These sharks** have flattened bodies. This allows them to stay close to the seabed. Most are about 1.5 m in length.

- **By burying themselves** on the seabed, angelsharks are hidden from passing fish and shellfish. They leap out to catch their prey with their small, sharp teeth.

- **Angelsharks can lie in wait** for over a week until their prey comes swimming past. One angelshark even managed to eat a cormorant – a type of large bird!

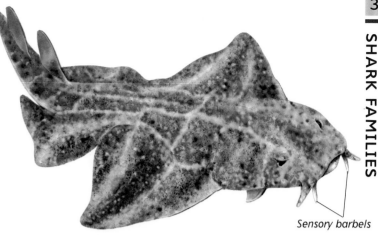

Sensory barbels

▲ *The angelshark has very rough skin on its back, and patches of small thorns on its snout and between its eyes.*

- **Female angelsharks** give birth to between one and 25 pups at a time.

- **Angelsharks** draw in water through their spiracles and pump it out over their gills to keep them from getting blocked with sand. Their gill openings are on the sides of their head, not underneath.

DID YOU KNOW?

The biggest angelshark, the Japanese angelshark, reaches lengths of 2 m or more.

Sawsharks

- **Part of an order** of eight shark species, sawsharks have flat heads and saw-shaped snouts. They spend most of their time swimming or resting on the seabed.

- **The snout is called a rostrum**. It is pointed and has teeth, called rostral teeth, of various sizes sticking out all the way around it.

- **The snout of the longnose sawshark** can make up one third of the total length of its body.

- **At around 70–150 cm** in length, sawsharks are relatively small.

- **Sawsharks** use their saws for digging up prey such as shellfish from the seabed. They slash and jab at their prey before eating it.

- **Two long barbels** halfway along the snout help the sawshark feel its way along the seabed.

- **Most sawsharks** are grey, but the Japanese sawshark is a muddy-brown colour.

DID YOU KNOW?

Sawsharks aren't usually seen near the shore. They prefer to live at depths of up to 400 m.

- **Sawsharks also** use their long saws for defence or for competing with rivals during courtship.

◄ *A sawshark hunts for food using its snout and sensitive barbels, which can feel, smell and taste its prey.*

- **Sixgill sawsharks** are the only sawsharks with six pairs of gill slits; other sawsharks have only five pairs. Sixgill sawsharks also have barbels closer to their mouths than other sawsharks, but are otherwise very similar.

- **Female sawsharks** give birth to between seven and 17 pups at a time. The large rostral teeth lie flat against the pups' snouts until after they are born, so they don't injure their mother.

Barbel

Rostral teeth

Dogfish sharks

● **The dogfish shark order** (Squaliformes), consists of about 130 species in six families: dogfish sharks, gulper sharks, lanternsharks, sleeper sharks, roughsharks and kitefin sharks.

● **These sharks** usually have spines in front of their dorsal fins and they have no anal fin.

● **They may have** been named 'dogfish' because they are the most common sharks or because many types move in large groups, like packs of wild dogs.

● **Female dogfish sharks** give birth to pups. A single litter may have anything from one to over 50 pups.

● **The spiny dogfish** has the longest known gestation period of any shark. Females can be pregnant for up to two years.

DID YOU KNOW?

In America, spiny dogfish used to be caught, dried and burned as a fuel.

● **The smalleye pygmy shark** is one of the smallest sharks. It measures less than 10 cm in length at birth.

● **Gulper sharks** have huge green or yellowish eyes to help them see in deep, dark waters, up to 1500 m deep.

● **Sleeper sharks** are named after their slow, sluggish swimming habits. The giant Pacific sleeper shark feeds on giant Pacific octopuses and also scavenges dead bodies in the deep sea.

● **The five species** of roughshark are named after their rough, tough skin. They have two high, triangular fins on the back, which look like the sails of a boat.

● **The kitefin shark** is an aggressive, deep-water predator, with powerful jaws and sharp teeth. The back edges of most of its fins are see-through.

◄ *A group of dogfish sharks on the prowl. They sometimes form schools of hundreds or even thousands of individuals.*

Greenland sharks

● **Although closely related** to dogfish, Greenland sharks are much bigger – they can grow up to around 6.5 m or more in length.

● **Greenland sharks** prefer cold water. They live in the north Atlantic, around Greenland, Iceland and Canada, and can stand temperatures as low as 2°C.

● **The Greenland shark** is a type of sluggish sleeper shark, which is related to another gigantic shark, the Pacific sleeper shark.

● **Alternative names** for the Greenland shark include ground shark, gurry shark, grey shark and sleeper shark. The Inuit name for this shark is Eqalussuaq.

● **Luminescent copepods** (tiny sea creatures) live in the eyes of the Greenland shark. They make the eyes glow in the dark, which may help lure prey towards the shark.

● **Greenland sharks eat fish**, squid, seals and sea lions, as well as scavenging on the dead bodies of whales.

▼ *One of the largest of all sharks, Greenland sharks are often characters in Inuit legends.*

● **In summer**, Greenland sharks swim to the surface to find food, but they spend the rest of their time at depths of around 1500 m.

● **Female Greenland sharks** give birth to between seven and ten pups at a time.

● **Inuits used to hunt** Greenland sharks on lines through iceholes. They used the skin to make boots, and the teeth for knife blades.

● **Fresh Greenland shark meat** is poisonous, but can be eaten safely if it is boiled several times.

DID YOU KNOW?

Greenland sharks are the longest-lived vertebrate animals on Earth.

Lanternsharks

● **Lanternsharks** are the largest family of dogfish sharks, with over 50 species.

● **They live throughout** the oceans, near the bottom, at depths of 200–1500 m.

● **Lanternsharks** are named after their ability to glow in the dark. They produce light from glowing spots called photophores on their bellies, sides and fins.

● **There can be** as many as 500,000 photophores on just one shark! In a photophore, two chemicals are combined, causing a reaction that gives off light.

● **Lanternsharks use hormones** to switch their light spots on and off. The hormones stimulate pigment (colour) cells to cover or uncover the light spots.

● **The light spots** may help to camouflage these sharks against lighter surface waters, or even allow them to signal to other lanternsharks and find a mate in dark water.

◀ *The photophores (glowing spots) form distinct black marks on the abdomen, sides or tail of some lanternsharks.*

● **Green dogfish** feed in groups. Their light patterns may help these sharks to find each other in murky water.

● **Some deep-sea lanternsharks**, such as the velvet belly shark, may use their lights to light up their surroundings in order to see prey.

● **The rough skin** of the granular dogfish is covered in denticles with sharp, hooked points, whereas the bareskin dogfish has a fragile, almost naked, skin with only a few, widely spaced denticles.

● **The lined lanternshark** has lines of dots and dashes along the top of its silvery-brown body, like Morse code.

● **The viper dogfish** has huge, curved, fang-like teeth to catch large fish, which it then swallows whole.

Cookie-cutter sharks

● **Found around the world**, cookie-cutter sharks are strange, deep-water sharks.

● **There are two species** – the cookie-cutter and the large-tooth cookie-cutter.

● **The large-tooth** is the smaller of the two, but it has bigger teeth. Its teeth are bigger in relation to its body size than those of any other shark.

● **Cookie-cutters** are brown in colour and have greenish eyes. They are about 50 cm in length.

● **To feed**, a cookie-cutter attaches itself to its prey by sucking with its mouth. Then it swivels its sharp teeth around in a circle until it has cut out a lump of flesh.

● **As cookie-cutters** don't need to catch their prey, they can feed on animals much larger than themselves.

● **Many sharks**, dolphins, porpoises and whales have permanent round scars from cookie-cutter shark bites.

● **The luminous underside** of the cookie-cutter shark can glow bright green and may help to attract its victims.

● **Although they are** relatively poor swimmers, cookie-cutter sharks probably migrate from deep water (2000–3000 m down) to mid-water levels or the surface at night.

DID YOU KNOW?

The cookie-cutter shark's Latin name, Isistius, comes from the Egyptian goddess of light, Isis.

▶ *The cookie-cutter has around 35 teeth in its upper jaw and 30 in its lower jaw.*

▲ *Cookie-cutters open their mouths wide to bite circular chunks out of their prey. They rarely kill their victims.*

Bullhead sharks

- **There are nine species** of bullhead sharks, including the horn shark, the Galapagos horn shark and the Port Jackson shark.

- **These stocky sharks** all have a pig-like snout and a small mouth in front of their eyes.

- **The prominent brow ridges** are polished smooth in species that rest by day in caves, or under ledges of rock or coral.

- **Bullhead sharks** are more active by night than by day.

- **They live in shallow coastal waters**, which are usually less than 100 m deep.

- **These sluggish sharks** wriggle slowly over the seabed hunting for prey, or clamber over the bottom on their paddle-like front fins.

- **Bullheads are small sharks**, growing to lengths of 1.2–1.7 m.

- **The sharp spines** on their back fins deter predators from trying to eat them.

- **Bullheads** have two different sorts of teeth. The pointed front teeth are used to hold prey, while the large, blunt back teeth are used for crushing shellfish and other small sea creatures.

- **Female bullhead sharks** lay eggs inside leathery egg cases, which are shaped like screws. They are such an awkward shape that it takes the mother several hours to lay each egg case.

◀ *A male crested bullhead shark eating the egg case of another species, a Port Jackson shark.*

Carpet sharks

- **The carpet sharks** are a varied group of about 40 different species of shark.

- **Species include blind sharks**, wobbegongs, nurse sharks, bamboo sharks and the zebra shark, as well as collared and long-tailed carpet sharks.

- **Many types** are less than one metre long, but this group also includes the whale shark, which is the biggest shark of all.

▼ *The large, dark 'eye spots' may help to startle a predator or stop a predator from attacking this epaulette shark's real eyes.*

- **They live** in warm tropical seas, such as those around Australia, Indonesia and Arabia, and often inhabit shallow waters around reefs and sandbars.

- **Carpet sharks** often lie still on the seabed. Many species have a slightly flattened body shape that helps to camouflage them.

- **Most carpet sharks** feed on crabs, shellfish, octopus and sea worms.

- **Some carpet sharks** lay eggs in cases, while others give birth to pups.

- **Many carpet sharks** have beautiful speckled markings, which resemble the patterns of carpets or tapestries.

- **Part of the long-tailed carpet shark family**, bamboo sharks use their leg-like, muscular fins to clamber over coral reefs.

- **Bamboo sharks can survive** out of water for up to half a day, allowing them to feed in small pools on coral or rocky reefs.

DID YOU KNOW?

Collared carpet sharks can change colour to match their surroundings.

Whale sharks

- **Whale sharks** are the biggest kind of shark and the largest fish on Earth. They grow to an enormous length of 14 m and have the same mass as a double-decker bus.

- **Their closest relatives** are zebra sharks and short-tail nurse sharks – not other filter-feeders such as basking sharks or megamouths.

- **The filter-feeding whale shark** sieves tiny plankton out of the water.

- **These huge sharks** are harmless to humans.

- **Although a whale shark** has around 3000 tiny teeth, they are of little use. Instead it uses bristles in front of its gills to trap food.

- **Scientists think** that some whale sharks could live to be 100 years old or more.

- **Whale sharks scoop up food** at or near the surface of the water, sometimes hanging vertically and bobbing up and down.

Huge mouth, up to 1.5 m across

▲ To catch food, a whale shark swims along with its massive mouth wide open.

- **The whale shark** has an extra-large liver full of oil to help it float more easily. Oil is lighter than water so this giant shark can swim slowly along at the surface of the sea without sinking.

- **A whale shark's liver** makes up about 20 percent of its body weight and may weigh as much as a small car.

- **One female whale shark** was found with 300 pups inside her.

Nurse sharks

- **Unlike most carpet sharks**, nurse sharks don't have carpet-like markings. They are usually brownish-grey, and sometimes have a few spots.

- **Nurse sharks** hunt at night. During the day, they often lie on the seabed in groups.

- **These large sharks** can reach 4 m in length.

- **Nurse sharks** have two barbels beneath their noses. They use them to smell and feel for prey.

- **With a preference** for warm, shallow water (usually up to about 12 m deep), nurse sharks can be found in the east Pacific Ocean and the Atlantic Ocean.

- **Crabs, lobsters and sea urchins** are the preferred food of nurse sharks. They have broad, flat teeth to grind up hard shells.

- **If a nurse shark bites**, it hangs on with a clamp-like grip. It can be almost impossible to dislodge it.

- **The nurse shark** uses its snout to find prey and sucks food in rapidly. It can even remove conch snails from their shells.

- **The tawny nurse shark** is also known as the spitting shark because it spits water at an attacker as a form of defence. After spitting, the tawny nurse shark is said to grunt. It is one of the few sharks thought to make a noise.

- **Females give birth** to between 20 and 30 pups at a time, after a pregnancy lasting six months.

◄ This nurse shark is using its strong pectoral fins to climb over rocks and coral on the seabed.

Wobbegongs

- **Wobbegong sharks**, also known as wobbies, belong to the carpet shark family.

- **The name 'wobbegong'** was given to these sharks by the Australian Aborigine people. It is thought that the word means 'shaggy beard'. Wobbegongs are often found in shallow, sandy water around the coast of Australia.

- **Wobbegongs can be quite large**, and some, such as the tasselled wobbegong, grow up to 4 m in length. They all have large, flattened bodies to help them hide on the seabed.

- **Wobbegongs have** lots of whisker-like barbels around their mouths. The barbels of the spotted wobbegong are branched and frilly.

- **The tasselled wobbegong** has tassel-like barbels around its face, like a beard.

- **Wobbegongs are powerful** seabed predators, feeding on smaller fish and other sea creatures, such as crabs, lobsters, octopus and squid. They suck in prey and spear it on their large teeth.

- **The strong jaws** of the wobbegong can easily bite off a person's hand or foot.

- **Wobbegongs sometimes bite** people who accidentally step on them. For this reason, they have a reputation as being dangerous. They may attack if they feel threatened.

- **Wobbegongs use** their strong fins to clamber around on the seabed, sometimes even moving out of the water.

- **The female spotted wobbegong** has large litters of up to 37 pups.

◄ *The beautiful gulf wobbegong lives on coral reefs around the coast of southern Australia. It sometimes attacks divers.*

Mackerel sharks

- **The mackerel shark** family consists of 15 species. They are mainly active, fast, open-ocean predators that live near the surface of the sea.

- **The most famous shark**, the great white, belongs to this family, as do mako, salmon and porbeagle sharks.

- **Two filter-feeders** – the megamouth shark and the basking shark – are also in the mackerel shark family.

- **One very unusual mackerel shark** is the goblin shark, with its sensitive, blade-like snout.

- **The diet of mackerel sharks** varies from dolphins, seals, birds and turtles, to other sharks, rays, fish and small sea creatures.

- **Some of the larger mackerel sharks**, such as the great white, sometimes attack people.

- **Many mackerel sharks** live in groups and some, such as thresher sharks, hunt together.

- **Some mackerel sharks**, such as the shortfin mako, migrate long distances.

- **Mackerel sharks** give birth to pups rather than laying eggs.

- **Most mackerel sharks** are threatened by over-fishing.

▼ *Measuring up to 3.5 m in length, the porbeagle shark is warm-blooded and a fast swimmer.*

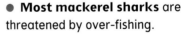

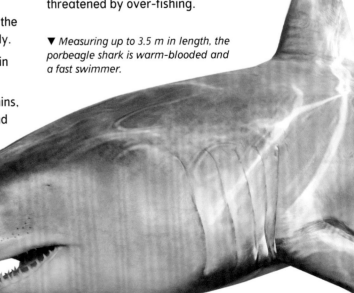

Goblin sharks

● **With its incredibly long**, flattened and pointed snout, the goblin shark looks very strange.

● **The long snout** looks like a weapon, but in fact, scientists think it helps the shark find prey using its sense of electrical detection.

● **Goblin sharks** have pale pink skin that is much softer and flabbier than the skin of most other sharks. It bruises easily.

● **Goblin sharks feed on fish**, squid and crustaceans such as crabs and lobsters.

● **Like many sharks**, the goblin shark pushes its jaws forwards as it attacks.

● **They have sharp teeth** at the front of their mouths for grabbing prey and smaller teeth at the back for chewing.

● **When they are born**, goblin sharks are 80–90 cm long, but they grow to lengths of at least 4 m.

◀ *Even when their jaws are not thrust out, goblin sharks are instantly recognizable by their flat, sharp-edged snouts and bubblegum-pink colour. The colour is due to many small blood vessels near to the surface of a partly see-through skin.*

● **Goblin sharks** live in the Atlantic, Pacific, and western Indian oceans.

● **The goblin shark's** large liver takes up 25 percent of its body weight, but scientists don't know why it is so big.

● **Scientists still do not know** much about these sharks as they are rarely caught.

DID YOU KNOW?

Goblin sharks have survived on Earth for millions of years without changing very much at all.

Megamouth sharks

● **One of the most recently discovered** sharks is the weird-looking megamouth. It is probably one of the rarest species.

● **The first known megamouth** was caught in 1976, off the islands of Hawaii.

● **The megamouth grows** to more than 5 m long. It has a very thick, rounded, heavy body and a huge head.

● **Megamouths are filter-feeders**. They feed at night, cruising near the surface with their mouths wide open to filter plankton out of the water.

● **During the day**, megamouths swim down to depths of 200 m or more.

● **The megamouth** gets its name due to its huge mouth, which can be up to 1.3 m wide.

DID YOU KNOW?

The inside of a megamouth's mouth may be silvery or reflective, or even glow-in-the-dark, in order to attract prey.

● **The scientific name** for the megamouth is *Megachasma pelagios*, which means 'huge yawner of the open sea'.

● **The mouth is at the front** of the snout, not underneath, as in most sharks.

● **The crocodile shark** is closely related to the megamouth shark but it is no bigger than a medium-sized dog and not a filter-feeder. Its main food is small fish, squid and shrimps, which it snaps up with its pointed teeth.

▼ *The megamouth traps small particles of food on finger-like bristles along its gills.*

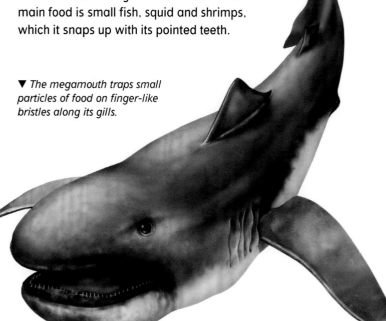

Sand tiger sharks

● **A typical sand tiger shark** is around 2–3 m long. It has brownish markings, but is not stripy like a tiger.

● **Sand tiger sharks** are not closely related to tiger sharks. They belong to a different order, and are more closely related to makos and great whites.

● **They are named after** their habit of swimming over the sandy seabed, and because of their large, sharp teeth.

● **Their diet is mainly fish**, but occasionally sand tigers kill and eat bigger animals such as sea lions.

● **The species is popular** in aquariums. They are exciting to watch and survive well in captivity.

▶ *A mouthful of sharp, pointed teeth helps the sand tiger shark to keep hold of slippery fish easily.*

● **The sand tiger shark** has lots of gaps between its irregular, projecting teeth, giving it a 'snaggle-tooth' appearance.

● **Sometimes**, sand tiger sharks feed together, surrounding prey to make it easier to catch.

● **Sand tiger sharks** can swallow air from the surface to help them hover at a particular depth in the water without using up a lot of their energy.

● **Male sand tiger sharks** guard females after mating, which gives their pups a better chance of surviving until they are born.

● **Female sand tiger sharks** give birth to two pups every other year after a pregnancy of between nine and 12 months. Pups hatch out of eggs inside the mother, and feed on the eggs and smaller pups that are produced after them.

Thresher sharks

● **There are three species** of thresher shark – the common, the pelagic and the bigeye.

● **Thresher sharks** are recognized by their extremely long tails. The upper lobe can be up to 50 percent of the shark's entire body length. Including the tail, these sharks can grow up to 6 m long.

● **They use their long tails** to round up shoals of small fish, such as sardines or herrings. Then they stun the fish by beating (or 'threshing') them with their tails before eating them.

● **Although threshers** are big, their mouths are small, so they only eat little prey.

● **Two or more thresher sharks** may work together to catch fish.

● **Thresher sharks** migrate away from the tropics to cooler waters in spring, and return to warmer waters in autumn.

● **Although thresher sharks** rarely attack humans, they have been known to injure fishermen by hitting them with their tails.

● **Common threshers** are the best-known sub-species, and are often seen near the seashore.

● **Pelagic threshers** get their name because they prefer to stay in the pelagic zone – the open sea – away from the seashore.

● **Bigeye threshers** often live in deep water. Their large eyes are up to 10 cm across – the size of a human fist!

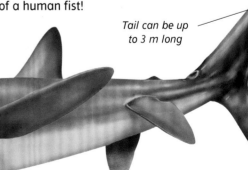

Tail can be up to 3 m long

▲ *Thresher sharks use their long tails to attack fish in two different ways. They either swim quickly forwards, then flick their tail sharply, or they swim alongside the fish and make a sideways strike with their tail.*

Basking sharks

● **Basking sharks** get their name because they appear to 'bask', or lie in the sun, close to the surface of the sea when they are feeding.

● **They are the second-biggest shark** after the whale shark, growing up to 12 m in length.

● **Basking sharks** are filter-feeders, and feed by sieving plankton out of the water.

● **These placid animals** do not attack humans. They lack big teeth for biting or chewing.

● **Basking sharks** will sometimes leap right out of the water, and then fall back down with a huge splash.

● **Other names** for this species are bone shark, elephant shark, bigmouth shark, or sunfish – because people used to think it enjoyed lying in the sun.

● **Occasionally, basking sharks** have been seen swimming in large groups of 50 or more.

● **Basking sharks** probably live for more than 50 years.

● **The basking shark** filters over 1.5 million litres of water in one hour. That's as much water as there is in an Olympic-sized swimming pool!

● **Unlike its cousin**, the great white, the basking shark is a gentle giant.

◀ *Basking sharks have enormous mouths up to one metre across, which they open widely when feeding. Their gill rakers are shed and re-grown at regular intervals.*

Great white sharks

● **The great white** is among the best-known of all sharks.

● **Belonging to the mackerel shark group**, great whites are fast, fierce hunters. They catch a wide variety of prey, from fish such as tuna, rays and smaller sharks, to marine mammals such as seals and dolphins, birds and turtles.

● **With large prey**, a great white may take a bite and then let go, leaving the animal to die from loss of blood before starting to feed.

● **A typical great white** is around 4–5 m long – slightly longer than a car. The biggest great whites on record were over 7 m long.

● **Great whites** are often found in medium-warm waters, such as those around Australia and Japan.

● **When swimming**, great whites will sometimes poke their heads out of the water or leap high into the air.

● **Great white sharks** are warm-blooded and keep a high body temperature, even in cold water.

● **This helps to speed up** their digestion, especially of fatty foods (such as seals), which are hard to digest but full of energy.

● **Female great whites** give birth to between two and 13 pups at a time after a pregnancy of about 12 months.

● **It is difficult** to keep a great white in captivity. If they are put into an aquarium, they live for only a few days.

▼ *A great white shark's body is sturdy, powerful and built for hunting.*

Mako sharks

● **Swift and fierce**, makos are strong, muscular hunting sharks that can swim at great speed.

● **One shortfin mako** travelled over 13,000 km in six months, swimming to and fro between New Zealand and Fiji.

● **Makos are closely related** to great whites, and they live and hunt in a similar way. They will sometimes attack humans, but their diet is predominantly fish.

▲ A fast-swimming, active shark, the short-finned mako has large eyes, a long, pointed snout and large, dagger-like teeth. Its crescent-shaped tail fin enables it to swim at high speed.

● **They have long**, streamlined, graceful bodies and pointed snouts, and can grow up to 4 m in length.

● **Known for their vivid colours**, makos are dark purple-blue on top and silvery-white underneath.

● **A mako's smooth teeth** are very narrow and pointed to help them grab slippery fish in their jaws.

● **The name 'mako'** comes from the Maori word for 'shark'. Makos are common around New Zealand, the home of the Maori people.

● **Female shortfin makos** have between four and 25 pups at a time. Each pup is about 70 cm long at birth.

● **People often fish makos** as sport and they are also caught for food.

Porbeagle sharks

● **Like great whites**, porbeagles are grey on top and white underneath. They also have a white mark on their dorsal fins.

● **Porbeagle sharks** grow up to 3 m in length. They have a second keel on their tails, which helps them to swim fast.

● **These sharks prefer** cooler seas, such as the north and south Atlantic Ocean. Porbeagles can keep their body temperature warmer than their surroundings.

● **Porbeagles are inquisitive** and may attack humans. However, attacks are rare because people don't usually venture into their cold water habitats.

● **Their diet is mostly fish** and squid. They will chase shoals of mackerel over long distances.

● **Porbeagles have long**, sharp teeth to spear prey and stop it from escaping.

● **Their smooth-edged teeth** cannot cut the flesh, so prey is usually swallowed whole.

● **Porbeagles migrate** with the seasons, moving to coastal waters near the shore in summer and swimming to deeper water for the winter months.

● **Female porbeagles** give birth to between one and five pups after a pregnancy of 8–9 months.

● **Porbeagles are among** the few fish that are thought to play. They roll over at the ocean surface, chase one another and wrap themselves in seaweed!

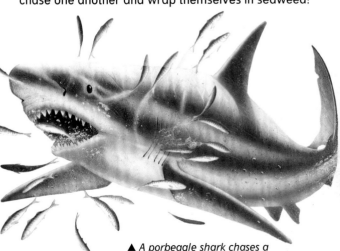

▲ A porbeagle shark chases a shoal of fast-swimming mackerel.

Catsharks

- **The largest shark family**, there are more than 160 species of catshark. Some have unusual names, including ghost catshark, bighead catshark, spongehead catshark and even Pinocchio catshark.

- **Catsharks are named** after their cat-like eyes.

- **They are usually** less than one metre in length, although some are only 30 cm long and a few reach 160 cm.

- **Catsharks eat** small fish and crabs.

- **Sometimes confused with dogfish**, catsharks can be identified by the lack of spines on their dorsal fins and are usually slimmer than dogfish.

- **Dogfish are usually** dull colours, but many catsharks have beautiful markings. The chain shark has patterns on its skin that look like silver chains.

- **Some catsharks** that live near the shore sleep in groups in rock crevices by day and come out at night.

- **Most catsharks lay eggs** in cases with long tendrils that curl round plants on the seabed.

- **A few catsharks**, such as the lollipop catshark and the African sawtail catshark, give birth to pups.

- **Catsharks are not dangerous** to people and some are kept in aquariums.

◄ *The coral catshark lives among the coral reefs of the western Pacific Ocean, from Pakistan and India to New Guinea and southern China. It hunts at night for small fish, shellfish and shrimp.*

Swellsharks

- **Also known as balloonsharks**, swellsharks are slow-moving sharks, about 50–100 cm in length.

- **This species** is named after its ability to swell to twice its normal size by pumping water into its stomach.

- **This ability** may startle or frighten a predator, giving a swellshark time to escape.

- **If in danger**, a swellshark puffs itself up into a ball inside a rocky crevice so it can't be pulled out of the rocks.

- **A closely related species**, the draughtsboard shark has dark and light checkerboard markings. It is said to bark like a dog as air escapes from its stomach.

- **Swellsharks** have long, wide mouths, which they use to gulp down mouthfuls of small fish before swallowing them whole.

- **They have up to 60 small, sharp teeth**, with dagger-like points, in each jaw.

- **Swellsharks catch prey**, such as small fish, in the dark by detecting the tiny electrical signals given off by the life processes of their prey.

- **Swellsharks hide in seaweed**, caves and rocky crevices by day and come out at night to hunt for fish, crabs, shrimps and prawns.

- **Very sociable**, swellsharks often rest together in groups during the day.

- **Female swellsharks** usually lay two eggs in large, purse-shaped egg cases.

▼ *The swellshark grows to a maximum length of about one metre. This sluggish shark is spotted and blotched all over, helping it to blend into a rocky seabed covered with seaweed.*

Houndsharks

- **There are more** than 40 species of houndshark, including the whiskery shark, the tope shark, the gummy shark and the leopard shark.

- **They are small** to medium-sized sharks, ranging from 40–150 cm in length.

- **Their oval eyes** have nictitating eyelids for protection.

- **Most types live** on shallow seabeds, but there are a few deep-water species that swim at great depths, possibly deeper than 2000 m.

- **The whiskery shark** is the only houndshark to have long barbels on its nose. These help it to catch octopuses, which are its preferred food.

▶ *A spotted houndshark swimming over a sandy seabed near the Galapagos Islands. These stout houndsharks also live along the coasts of Peru and northern Chile.*

- **Instead of sharp, biting teeth**, most houndsharks have flat teeth for crushing prey, such as shellfish, crabs and lobsters.

- **Gummy sharks** were named because they seemed to have no teeth. They actually have flat, grinding teeth instead of sharp, pointy ones.

- **Female houndsharks** give birth to between one and 52 pups.

- **Tope sharks** may make long migration journeys to find food or safe places to have their young.

- **The leopard shark** may form schools with smoothhound sharks, spiny dogfish and bat rays.

Weasel sharks

- **Most weasel shark** species are small, usually no more than one metre in length.

- **There are about** eight different species, including the hooktooth, the snaggletooth and the sicklefin weasel shark.

- **Weasel sharks live** in coastal waters of the east Atlantic Ocean and the west of the Pacific Ocean.

- **They have oval eyes** with nictitating eyelids, which they can draw across their eyes for protection.

- **The hooktooth shark** has very long, hooked lower teeth, which stick out from its long mouth.

- **Straight-tooth weasel sharks** have pointed lower teeth, but they do not stick out of the short, arched mouth.

- **The Atlantic weasel shark** has a specialized diet of squid and octopuses.

- **It has a striking pattern** of yellow stripes along its back, which is light grey or bronze.

- **The female snaggletooth shark** gives birth to between two and 11 pups at a time, after a pregnancy of seven to eight months.

- **Most weasel sharks** are harmless to humans, apart from the snaggletooth shark, which is large enough to be a threat. It reaches a maximum length of 2.4 m.

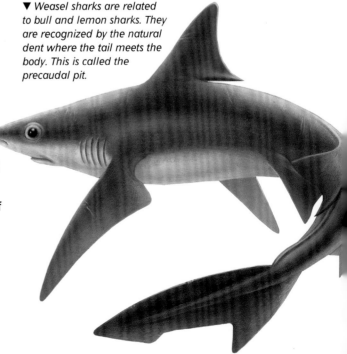

▼ *Weasel sharks are related to bull and lemon sharks. They are recognized by the natural dent where the tail meets the body. This is called the precaudal pit.*

Requiem sharks

● **There are at least** 56 species in the requiem shark family (Carcharhinidae). It was probably named after the French word for shark, *requin*.

● **The family includes** some of the most typical and well-known sharks, such as blue sharks, lemon sharks, tiger sharks, bull sharks and reef sharks.

● **Requiem sharks** are sometimes called whaler sharks.

● **Sharks in this family** are usually large and chunky-looking, with bodies 1–3 m long.

● **Their skin** is usually plain, without any patterns, although they are dark on top and light beneath. This countershading camouflages them from above and below.

● **Sharks in this family** have long, arched mouths with sharp, blade-like teeth.

● **Their eyes** are usually round with nictitating eyelids.

● **They have two fins** on their back. The second dorsal fin is usually smaller, and the top lobe of their tail fin is much larger than the bottom lobe.

▲ *The bull shark is a fierce predator, which attacks animals as large as cattle and hippos. Smaller prey includes baby sharks, such as lemon shark and sandbar shark pups.*

● **Most requiem sharks** live in tropical waters, both near the shore and out in the open ocean, with most living in sunlit surface waters rather than the deep ocean.

● **A few requiem sharks** – the bull shark and the river sharks – are the only shark species that can live in freshwater for long periods of time.

> **DID YOU KNOW?**
> Bull sharks living in rivers produce 20 times more urine than those living in the sea.

Blue sharks

● **The streamlined shape** and long front fins of the blue shark allow it to move very fast through the oceans when hunting prey.

● **Named after its deep**, silvery-indigo colour on top, this shark has a pale underside.

● **Blue sharks** sometimes swim at the surface but reach depths of up to 335 m.

● **These sharks eat** mostly squid, although they will feed on any kind of fish or other sea creature.

● **The blue shark** has large, sensitive eyes to find prey and finger-like bristles on its gills to stop small prey escaping from its gill slits.

● **It may circle** round swimmers, boats and divers for some time before closing in and biting.

● **The skin of a female blue shark** is twice as thick as that of the male. This helps to protect the females from bites during courtship and mating.

● **This species** was once extremely common, and is found in almost every part of every ocean. The population is now falling because it is so heavily overfished.

● **Blue sharks** are often caught by accident on hooks or in nets intended for tuna and swordfish.

● **Experts have estimated** that ten million blue sharks are caught and killed every year.

▼ *Blue sharks are sleek, slim and graceful, and grow up to 4 m in length.*

> **DID YOU KNOW?**
> Blue sharks have large litters of pups, sometimes giving birth to more than 100 at a time.

Tiger sharks

- **The tiger shark** will attack almost anything, including humans, making it one of the most dangerous sharks.

- **These sharks** are usually about 3 m long, but they can grow up to 6 m.

- **They have massive heads** with a blunt snout, large eyes and a wide mouth.

- **The diet of tiger sharks** includes fish, seals, sea lions, turtles, shellfish, crabs, seabirds, dolphins, crocodiles, squid and jellyfish. They also take bites out of bigger animals such as whales, and have even been seen eating other tiger sharks.

- **Many unusual objects**, such as oil drums, tin cans, glass bottles, clothes, rubber tyres, coal, cushions, tools, and even pieces of armour, have been found in the stomachs of tiger sharks.

- **This species** is found in most of the world's warmer seas and oceans. It sometimes swims into river mouths.

- **Tiger sharks** are named after the striped markings of the young, which fade with age.

▲ *Tiger sharks usually hunt alone, swimming slowly through the oceans until they spot a potential meal. This tiger shark is swimming in front of a group of lemon sharks, fighting for their share of food.*

- **Females have large numbers** of pups – 35–55 pups at a time are common, but up to 82 pups may be born at one time.

- **Tiger sharks are strong swimmers**, able to reach speeds of more than 32 km/h in just a few seconds. However, they cannot swim this fast for very long.

- **Some tiger sharks** may travel many thousands of kilometres in one year, while others keep to a small stretch of coastline just 100 km long.

Bull sharks

- **The bull shark** is a powerful, aggressive hunter. It gets its name because its body is thick, stocky and muscular, like a bull.

- **This species** is not especially long – bull sharks usually grow to between 2–3 m in length.

- **They are among** the few species that can survive in fresh water. Bull sharks swim hundreds of kilometres up rivers such as the Mississippi in North America, the Amazon in South America and the Zambezi in Africa.

▼ *A very short, wide head, blunt snout and small eyes are characteristic features of the bull shark.*

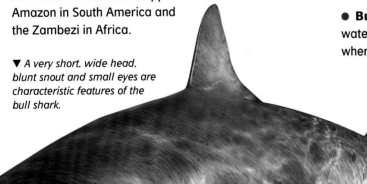

- **Some bull sharks** have been found living in Lake Nicaragua, a large lake in Central America.

- **Bull sharks** are often known by other names, depending on where they live – such as the Zambezi River shark or the Nicaragua shark.

- **Some experts think** that bull sharks may be the most dangerous species. This is because they often lurk in shallow waters where humans swim.

- **Bull sharks** usually swim slowly near the seabed in water less than 20 m deep, but they are agile and quick when chasing prey.

- **They eat a wide range** of food, from fish and sea turtles to birds, dolphins and dead whales.

- **Bull sharks** have small eyes because they often live in shallow, muddy waters, where eyesight is not that useful for hunting prey.

- **Fierce and strong**, bull sharks probably attack more people than any other shark. They have huge jaws and large, sharp teeth.

Blacktip reef sharks

- **Blacktip reef sharks** have black tips on all their fins and are sometimes known as black sharks.

- **The black fin tips** may help to break up the shark's outline and improve its camouflage.

- **Like its cousin** the whitetip reef shark, the blacktip prefers warm, shallow water.

- **This shark has long**, slender teeth ideally suited to snapping up its main prey – fish that live around coral reefs.

- **Adults usually grow** to lengths of about one metre but some reach maximum lengths of up to 2 m.

- **Blacktip reef sharks** have small, oval eyes with a pupil like a vertical slit. Their eyes don't need to let in much light as they live in shallow, sunlit waters.

- **They are strong, active** swimmers, and their back fin often breaks through the surface in shallow water.

- **Blacktip reef sharks live** in the western Pacific Ocean, the Indian Ocean and the eastern Mediterranean.

- **They live alone** or in very small groups.

- **Females give birth** to between two and four pups at a time, after a pregnancy lasting 16 months.

▼ The black fin markings of the blacktip reef shark contrast strongly with its pale skin.

Black tip to dorsal fin

DID YOU KNOW?

Since the Suez Canal was built, blacktip reef sharks have been able to swim through it from the Red Sea to the Mediterranean Sea.

Spinner sharks

- **This very active shark** is named after the way it spins through schools of fish with its mouth open when feeding.

- **It spins right out** of the water at the end of a feeding run, turning round and round up to three times before falling back into the water.

- **As well as fish**, spinner sharks also eat stingrays, squid and octopuses.

- **They have narrow**, pointed teeth in both jaws to help them keep a tight grip on slippery fish.

- **The narrow**, pointed snout of the spinner shark helps it to swim quickly and catch speedy fish.

- **Spinner sharks live** in warm to hot waters in the Atlantic Ocean, Mediterranean Sea and the western Pacific Ocean.

- **In the Gulf of Mexico**, Spinner sharks migrate towards the shore to feed and breed as the water warms up in spring. In winter, they move into deeper water and may also travel further south.

- **Young spinner sharks** prefer lower water temperatures to the adults.

- **Females give birth** to between three and 15 pups at a time, after a pregnancy of 11–15 months.

- **Adult and young spinner sharks** have obvious black tips to most of their fins.

▼ The spinner shark is sometimes confused with the blacktip shark because of its black fin tips. It has long gill slits in front of its pectoral fins.

Night sharks

- **The night shark** is a deepwater shark, found at depths of between 275–365 m during the day, and 185 m at night.

- **There are no recorded attacks** on humans by this species.

- **The night shark** has a very long, pointed snout that is longer than the width of its mouth.

- **These sharks** live off the east coast of the Americas, from the USA south to Argentina, as well as off the west coast of Africa.

- **Although similar in appearance** to silky sharks and dusky sharks, unlike the night shark, neither of these species has green eyes.

- **Night sharks** are slim, grey-brown sharks, with small dorsal and pectoral fins.

- **There are 15 rows of teeth** on each side of the night shark's top and bottom jaws. The triangular top teeth have jagged edges, while the bottom teeth are narrow and upright.

- **The night shark feeds** on squid and small fish, including flying fish and sea bass.

- **Females give birth** to between 12 and 18 pups at a time. The pups are 60–72 cm long at birth.

- **Adults grow** to about 2 m long, reaching maximum lengths of 2.8 m.

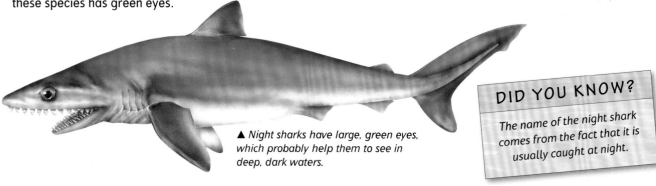

▲ Night sharks have large, green eyes, which probably help them to see in deep, dark waters.

DID YOU KNOW?

The name of the night shark comes from the fact that it is usually caught at night.

River sharks

- **Only a handful of sharks** (about six species) can survive in the freshwater of rivers.

- **River sharks** live in parts of south and southeast Asia, and Australia. They grow up to 3 m in length.

- **River sharks** include the Borneo river shark, the Ganges shark, the New Guinea river shark, the speartooth shark and the Irrawaddy river shark.

- **All of these sharks** are very rare and in danger of dying out.

- **This is probably due** to people damaging their habitat and catching too many fish in the rivers where they live.

- **River sharks** have tiny eyes because eyesight is not an important sense in muddy river water. These sharks probably rely more on their electrical senses than their eyes.

- **The speartooth shark** is named after the tips of its lower teeth, which are shaped like tiny spears. The spear-like tips of the teeth have sharp cutting edges.

- **The eyes of the Ganges shark** point upwards. As it swims along the riverbed looking for prey, its upward-facing eyes may help it to search for prey in the water above.

- **River sharks** are secretive, mysterious creatures and scientists know very little about them.

- **They probably** use their small, pointed teeth to catch fish.

- **Female river sharks** probably give birth to pups, but little is known about the details of their reproduction.

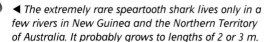

◀ The extremely rare speartooth shark lives only in a few rivers in New Guinea and the Northern Territory of Australia. It probably grows to lengths of 2 or 3 m.

Hammerhead sharks

● **Hammerheads** are probably the strangest-looking sharks. The head is extremely wide and the eyes are at either end of the flat, streamlined hammer.

● **A hammerhead shark** has to turn its head from side to side in order to see forwards.

● **Experts think this head shape** may help the shark to find food (such as fish, other sharks, rays, squid and octopuses), by spreading out their ampullae of Lorenzini over a wide area.

● **The shark's nostrils** are also spread wide apart on its head, giving it 'stereo-sniffing' power and helping it to detect the scent of prey.

● **The hammer-shaped head** also works like underwater 'wings' to lift the shark upwards as it moves through the water.

● **There are nine species** of hammerhead, including great, scalloped, smooth, winghead and bonnethead sharks. Each species has a head of a slightly different size and shape.

▲ *A bonnethead shark swallows a ray it has just found partially buried in the sandy seabed. It isn't affected by the ray's painful sting.*

▼ *The smooth hammerhead does not have a notch in the middle of its hammer-shaped head.*

DID YOU KNOW?

The great hammerhead is the biggest hammerhead shark and can grow up to 6 m in length.

● **During the day**, hammerhead sharks can often be seen swimming in large groups.

● **In hammerhead shark groups**, larger sharks tend to swim in the safest places in the middle of the group and smaller sharks around the outside. The sharks control their position in the group with displays, such as head shakes and swimming in large loops.

● **Hammerheads have taller dorsal fins** and smaller pectoral fins than most other sharks. This helps them to feed on the seabed.

● **Hammerhead females** give birth to pups. Scalloped hammerheads have 13–31 pups at a time after a pregnancy lasting eight to twelve months.

Shark relatives

● **Sharks are closely related** to two other groups of fish – the batoids and the chimaeras.

● **The batoids** include rays, skates, sawfish and guitarfish. They range in size from plate-sized skates to giant manta rays.

● **There are more** than 550 species of batoids – more than the number of shark species.

● **Most batoids** have wide, flat heads and bodies, and long, tapering tails. They look similar to some types of shark, such as angelsharks.

● **Most batoids feed** on bottom-dwelling sea creatures, such as clams, shrimps and flatfish, although manta rays feed on plankton and pelagic stingrays feed on squid.

● **Most batoids swim** by flapping their large, front fins. Some, such as sawfish, guitarfish and torpedo rays, use their tail for swimming, as sharks do.

▶ *The smalltooth sawfish reaches an average length of 5.5 m.*

● **Sharks are often difficult to catch** and keep in captivity, so scientists often study batoids instead. They are very similar to sharks, so they can provide clues to how sharks live.

● **Chimaeras are strange-looking**, long-tailed fish. Their name means 'a mixture', as they look a little like a cross between a shark and a bony fish.

● **The various species** of chimaera are also known as ratfish, ghost sharks, spook fish and even ghouls.

● **Like sharks**, batoids and chimaeras have light, flexible skeletons made of cartilage, instead of bone like other fish.

Rays

● **Rays are a type of batoid**. They are closely related to sharks.

● **Some rays** are wider than they are long because of their huge, flat, wing-like fins.

● **Most rays** use their wing-like pectoral fins for swimming. They look as if they are 'flying' underwater.

● **Many rays have** a long, whip-like tail. Unlike sharks, they don't use their tails to push themselves through the water.

● **Most rays are ovoviviparous** – they give birth to live young that have hatched from eggs inside the mothers' bodies, like some sharks do.

● **Rays live in seas** and oceans all around the world, from shallows near the shore to seabeds 3000 m deep.

● **Most species** are solitary and prefer to live alone. However some, such as golden cow-nosed rays, form huge groups of thousands of individuals.

● **There are two species** of manta ray – the giant oceanic manta and the smaller reef manta. In both species, the wingspan is about twice the length of the body.

● **Manta rays** have a docile nature and are preyed on by killer whales and large sharks, such as the great white shark.

● **Many rays** have colourful patterns on their skin and live in shallow water. The Australian leopard whipray has leopard-like spots on its skin.

▼ *Rays have wide, flat bodies, which helps them to skim closely along the seabed, searching for food.*

Electric rays

- **Electric rays** can generate electricity to give other animals a powerful electric shock. This ability can be used to deter predators or stun prey.

- **Some electric rays** produce as little as 37 volts or less, while Atlantic torpedo rays can generate as much as 220 volts of electricity.

- **The ancient Greeks** used the electricity from electric rays to numb the pain of operations and childbirth.

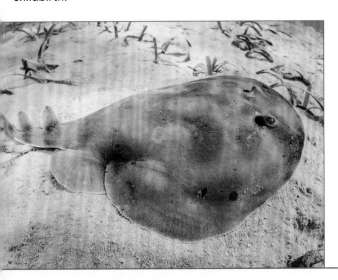

DID YOU KNOW?

The mouth of the Australian coffin ray is gigantic, which allows it to swallow prey half the size of its own body!

- **Short-nose electric rays** include some of the smallest rays, at less than 20 cm across. They are about the size of a pancake!

- **There are over 60 species** of electric ray, including Atlantic torpedo rays, the lesser electric ray and the marbled electric ray.

- **Electric rays** live in shallow waters, but can also be found in waters at least 1000 m deep.

- **Most electric rays** bury themselves under sand on the seabed during the day and come out at night to feed.

- **Electric rays feed** on fish, worms and shellfish. Adult Atlantic rays eat eels, flounders and even small sharks.

- **Lesser electric rays** have two pups at a time, while Atlantic torpedo rays may have as many as 60 pups at a time.

◄ A lesser electric ray lives in shallow coastal waters. It can generate a voltage of 14–37 volts in order to stun prey or defend itself from predators.

Stingrays

- **Stingrays have a poisonous spine** (or sometimes two or three) in the middle of their tails. It is used mainly for defence against attack.

- **River stingrays**, unlike other rays, live in freshwater. They are found in rivers in Africa and South America, especially the Amazon River.

- **Round stingrays** have almost completely round, flat bodies, like dinner plates.

- **Spotted eagle rays** are covered with beautiful pale spots on dark skin, but are white underneath.

- **Most stingrays** live on the seabed. They feed on shellfish and crabs, which they crush with their teeth.

- **The eagle, duckbilled and cownose rays** are nicknamed 'nutcracker rays'. This is because their teeth are joined together to form plates, which they use to crush their hard-shelled prey.

DID YOU KNOW?

A group of stingrays is called a 'fever' of stingrays.

- **Most stingrays** only attack people in self-defence. If a person accidentally steps on a stingray buried in the sand, the stingray may flip up its dangerous tail to stab the person's legs or ankles with poison.

- **Females give birth** to between five and 15 young after a pregnancy of about nine months.

- **The mothers feed** the young a sort of 'milk' while they are developing inside their uterus (womb).

- **The pelagic stingray** is different. It lives in the open ocean and feeds mainly on squid.

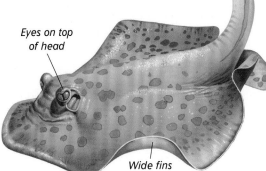
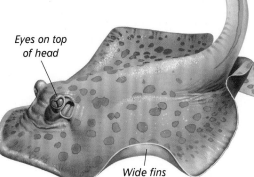

Long tail

Spines

Eyes on top of head

► The bright blue spots of the blue-spotted stingray warn other animals that it has poisonous tail spines.

Wide fins

Skates

- **Skates are similar to rays**, but they tend to have straighter edges to the front of their pectoral fins, and shorter tails.

- **Most types of skate** live in deep water, as far down as 3000 m.

- **Skates usually lie** on the seabed waiting for prey such as crabs and shrimps to come close.

- **As its mouth** is on its underside, a skate does not lunge at its prey. Instead it swims over the victim and grasps it from above.

- **Like some sharks**, skates lay eggs with protective cases.

- **The egg cases** of the flapper skate are up to 25 cm long, and each contains as many as seven eggs.

- **Skate egg cases** have stiff spikes to help them stick into the seabed. They also have a sticky coating so that they soon become covered with sand or pebbles as a form of camouflage.

- **Skate is a popular food** in some parts of the world – especially the fins, which are called 'skate wings'.

- **The largest skate** is the flapper skate, which reaches lengths of up to 2.8 m.

- **The Texas skate** has two big spots, one on each 'wing'. These spots look like the eyes of a larger animal, and may deter predators.

◀ *The common skate can be recognized by its long and pointed snout. This species is now usually called the flapper skate.*

DID YOU KNOW?

The flapper skate is critically endangered due to over-fishing and habitat destruction.

Guitarfish

- **Guitarfish** are a family of rays with over 40 different species.

- **The head** of a guitarfish is long, flat and guitar-shaped unlike the disc-shaped head of other rays.

- **The front fins** are smaller than those of other rays and they use their tails for swimming (like sharks).

- **The giant guitarfish** reaches lengths of up to 3 m. It is found in the Red Sea and Indian Ocean.

- **During the day**, the shovelnose guitarfish lays buried in the sand, with only its eyes sticking out, waiting to ambush crabs or flatfish. At night, it swims over the seabed, hunting for crabs, worms and clams.

- **Shovelnose guitarfish** crush crabs and shellfish with their many rows of pebble-like teeth.

- **The bowmouth guitarfish** (also known as the sharkfin guitarfish) has a mouth shaped like a longbow, and heavy ridges of sharp, spiky thorns on its head for defence.

- **It uses its large head** and front fins to trap prey against the seabed, then quickly gulps down its meal.

- **Female sharkfin guitarfish** have four to nine pups at a time. Each pup is about 45 cm long.

- **Young sharkfin guitarfish** have spots and bars on their skin, which gives them better camouflage than the adults, which are mainly grey.

DID YOU KNOW?

The shovelnose guitarfish has been living on our planet for over 100 million years.

▶ *The mottled, yellow-brown colours of the shovelnose guitarfish help it to blend into its sandy seabed habitat.*

Sawfish

● **The seven species** of sawfish are a type of ray.

● **Sawfish get their name** from their long, saw-like snouts called rostrums, which are edged with sharp teeth, like those on a saw.

● **The green sawfish** grows to more than 7 m in length – longer than a great white shark.

● **Its saw** can account for up to one third, or more, of a sawfish's length.

● **Like rays**, sawfish have flattened bodies, but they look more like sharks than most rays do.

● **Although sawfish** resemble sawsharks, they are not the same. Sawfish are much bigger and lack barbels on their saws.

● **A sawfish uses** its saw to poke around the seabed for prey and to slice into shoals of fish.

● **When young sawfish** are born, their snouts are soft and enclosed in a covering of skin. This protects the inside of the mother's body from being injured by their sharp teeth. After birth, the protective skin soon falls off and the saw hardens.

● **The large-tooth sawfish** sometimes swims up rivers in Australia.

● **All species of sawfish** are endangered, due to over-fishing by people and habitat destruction of coastal regions, such as mangrove swamps, where they live.

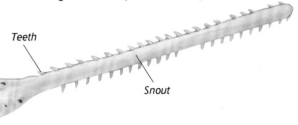

Teeth

Snout

▲ *The sawfish's snout is the same width all the way along, with a gently curved tip.*

Chimaeras

● **Although they are related** to sharks and rays, chimaeras have evolved separately for nearly 400 million years.

● **There are over 40 species** of chimaeras. They live in water ranging from 500–2500 m beneath the surface.

● **The elephant fish** is a type of chimaera with a long, fleshy snout, which it uses to detect the electrical signals given off by buried shellfish.

● **Chimaeras have a plate-like gill cover** over their four gills (like bony fish).

● **To swim**, they flap their wing-like front fins, like rays.

● **Unlike sharks**, chimaeras cannot replace any teeth that are worn out or broken.

▲ *The spotted ratfish has large eyes and long fins. Unlike many sharks and rays, chimaeras swim very slowly. They stay close to the seabed, feeding on small fish and octopuses.*

● **With plate-like**, grinding teeth and large nostrils, a chimaera's mouth looks like that of a rabbit. Another of their nicknames is rabbitfish.

● **The eyes of chimaeras** are usually green and very large, which helps them to pick up as much light as possible in the deep sea.

● **Most chimaeras** have a poisonous spine in front of their back fin.

● **Females lay eggs** with leathery egg cases.

◀ *The elephant fish has large green eyes high up on its head, and large front fins, which it uses for swimming.*

ELECTRIC RAYS

Cerebellum

Nerves

Right electric organ

Left electric organ

Spinal cord

Electric rays generate and store electricity in kidney-shaped electric organs (rather like batteries) at the base of their front fins. They use their electricity to stun their prey, defend themselves from predators and communicate with each other.

Inside a ray

With their wide, flat bodies and wing-like fins, rays look very different from most sharks. They are nearly all adapted for living on the seabed, where they feed on shellfish, shrimps and worms. Unlike sharks, which use their tails for swimming, rays swim by flapping their pectoral fins up and down like wings, or by rippling the edges of these fins.

On the inside, a ray's body is supported by a skeleton made from flexible cartilage, or gristle, just like a shark's skeleton. A ray also has gills to absorb oxygen from the water and similar internal organs to a shark. It has a large, oily liver, which helps it to float because oil is lighter than water. The fat in its liver also provides a useful source of stored energy. A ray's digestive system consists of a tube from its mouth leading to a stomach, a short intestine (gut) and an opening called the cloaca for wastes to pass out.

Manta ray from below

▲ MANTA RAY
Manta rays are the largest rays, measuring up to 7 m across their giant fins. They sometimes make spectacular leaps out of the water, crashing back with a splash that can be heard from many kilometres away. Mantas may do this to communicate with other mantas, to show off their fitness, or as part of a courtship display. A manta's leaps may also help it to escape predators or get rid of pesky parasites that irritate its skin.

▼ ABOVE AND BELOW
A ray has eyes and breathing holes (spiracles) on top of its body. Underneath its body are its mouth, gills slits and nostrils (nares). When they are buried in sand or mud on the seabed, rays use their spiracles to pump water to their gills, so they can keep breathing. This means they do not need to open the mouth to take in water and end up choking on mouthfuls of sand or mud.

Electric ray

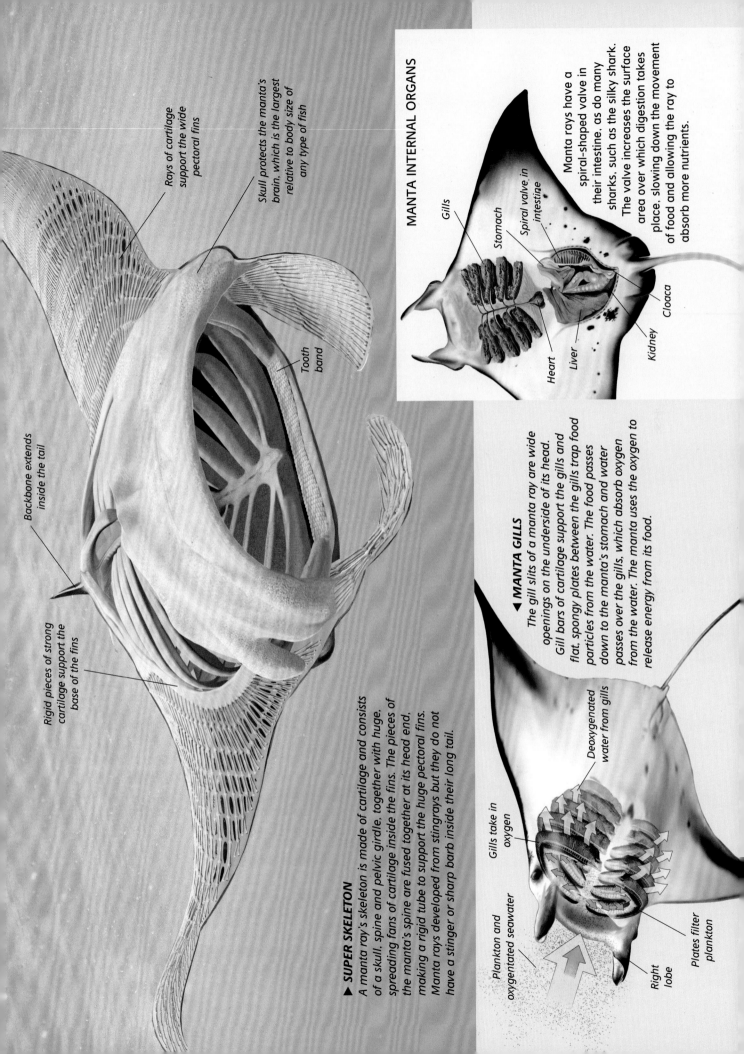

MANTA INTERNAL ORGANS

Gills

Stomach

Spiral valve in intestine

Heart

Liver

Kidney

Cloaca

Manta rays have a spiral-shaped valve in their intestine, as do many sharks, such as the silky shark. The valve increases the surface area over which digestion takes place, slowing down the movement of food and allowing the ray to absorb more nutrients.

Rays of cartilage support the wide pectoral fins

Skull protects the manta's brain, which is the largest relative to body size of any type of fish

Backbone extends inside the tail

Rigid pieces of strong cartilage support the base of the fins

Tooth band

► SUPER SKELETON

A manta ray's skeleton is made of cartilage and consists of a skull, spine and pelvic girdle, together with huge, spreading fans of cartilage inside the fins. The pieces of the manta's spine are fused together at its head end, making a rigid tube to support the huge pectoral fins. Manta rays developed from stingrays but they do not have a stinger or sharp barb inside their long tail.

◄ MANTA GILLS

The gill slits of a manta ray are wide openings on the underside of its head. Gill bars of cartilage support the gills and flat, spongy plates between the gills trap food particles from the water. The food passes down to the manta's stomach and water passes over the gills, which absorb oxygen from the water. The manta uses the oxygen to release energy from its food.

Gills take in oxygen

Deoxygenated water from gills

Plankton and oxygenated seawater

Right lobe

Plates filter plankton

Dangerous or not?

● **It's a natural instinct** for people to be scared of sharks, as some are fierce hunters. Although sharks can be dangerous, attacks on humans are rare.

● **As well as attacking humans**, great whites have been known to attack small boats.

● **Great whites are deadly** to humans partly because we look similar in size and shape to their prey – seals and sea lions. The sharks simply get confused and attack the wrong prey.

● **Many experts think** bull sharks are actually more dangerous than great whites – but they are not well-known as killers because they are harder to identify. After an attack, bullsharks often escape unseen.

● **Sharks with spines**, such as horn and dogfish sharks, are not deadly but can inflict painful injuries on people.

● **Not all dangerous sharks** are fast hunters. Nurse sharks and wobbegongs are usually placid and sluggish animals – but they can bite suddenly and hard if disturbed.

● **Stingrays**, which are related to sharks, can be killers – a few people die every year from their venom.

● **The wildlife expert** and TV personality Steve Irwin was killed in 2006, when a stingray barb pierced his heart while he was filming an underwater documentary.

● **Of the many hundreds** of shark species, only about 12 are usually dangerous to people. The top four are the great white, the bull shark, the tiger shark and the oceanic whitetip shark.

● **Other dangerous sharks** are the great hammerhead, shortfin mako, porbeagle, sand tiger shark, Galapagos shark, blacktip shark, Caribbean reef shark and grey reef shark.

◀ *More people have been killed by the box jellyfish than sharks and crocodiles combined. This lethal jellyfish can kill a person in just a few minutes.*

Attacks and survival

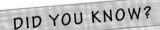

● **Every year** there are fewer than 100 reported cases worldwide of sharks attacking humans. Of these attacks, fewer than 20 are fatal.

● **Most attacks happen** in shallow water near the shore. This is because that's where sharks and swimmers are most likely to be in the same place at the same time.

● **Most incidents** happen off the coasts of eastern North America, South Africa and eastern Australia.

● **The danger of a shark attack** increases at night, when sharks move inshore to feed and are most active.

● **Sharks usually only attack** if they are hungry, if they feel threatened or angry, or if they mistake a human for prey. Divers may provoke an attack if they grab a shark by the tail.

● **People are more likely** to be killed by a lightning strike than a shark attack. Bees, wasps and snakes also kill many more people than sharks every year.

● **There are more deaths** from car accidents in one month than shark attacks in recorded history.

● **A great white shark** bit off marine photographer Henri Bource's leg while he was diving off the coast of Australia in 1964. He was soon back at work in the same job, and four years later another shark bit his artificial leg.

● **In 2003**, 13-year old Bethany Hamilton had her left arm bitten off by a tiger shark while surfing in Hawaii. She was surfing again within months and is still a top surfer.

● **In 2004**, while snorkelling in Australia, Luke Tresoglavic was bitten by a wobbegong. He had to swim to shore and drive to get help with the shark still attached.

◀ *Bethany Hamilton is still a top surfer, despite losing an arm in a tiger shark attack.*

Studying sharks

● **We know relatively little** about sharks. Scientists are trying to find out more about them.

● **The study of sharks** is sometimes called elasmobranchology.

● **Knowing more about sharks** – such as how they breed and what they need to survive – will help us to conserve them and stop shark species from dying out.

● **If you'd like to be a shark scientist**, choose subjects such as biology and chemistry at school, and study biology, genetics, oceanography or zoology at university.

● **Scientists also catch sharks** so they can study them in captivity. This lets them look closely at how sharks swim, eat and behave.

● **In laboratories**, scientists study shark blood, skin and cartilage to find out how their bodies work.

● **Some scientists study shark cells** to try to find out why they get so few diseases. This information could help to make new medicines.

● **In aquariums**, scientists test shark reactions to see how their brains and senses work.

● **Genetic analysis** of shark DNA helps scientists to identify closely related shark species, which look very similar and are difficult to distinguish from their appearance alone.

● **Dried shark tissue** from ancient sharks in museums can even be examined genetically to confirm the species and find out more about sharks that lived hundreds of years ago.

◀ *Some sharks, such as great whites, take an interest in diving cages, and seem to become more familiar with humans after coming into contact with them.*

Observation

● **To learn more about sharks**, scientists need ways of finding, following and catching them.

● **Most shark scientists** have to be strong and good at diving to get up close.

● **Scientists often use** diving cages or protective chainmail suits to study sharks underwater.

● **They can also study sharks** such as great whites without going in the water, using cameras on the ends of long poles.

● **Some shark scientists** dissect dead sharks to find out about their bodies or what they have eaten recently.

● **To follow sharks**, scientists use radio-tracking devices. They catch a shark and attach a transmitter that gives out radio signals. Wherever the shark goes, scientists can pick up the signals and work out the shark's location.

● **Scientists sometimes** attach tags to sharks they catch. The tag states where and when the shark was last caught. The same shark may then be found again somewhere else, giving scientists information about the shark's range.

▲ *A diver swims alongside a shark and records its movements and activities.*

● **A camera can be attached** to a shark to record its travels. The strap holding the camera gradually dissolves, and the camera floats to the surface to be collected.

● **Satellite tags** help scientists to track shark migration journeys by reporting the position of the shark to the satellite whenever the shark comes to the ocean's surface.

● **There is no evidence** that fitting scientific tags to a shark affects its survival in the wild.

Early sharks

● **The first fish** with a shark-like body shape lived about 450 million years ago. They were not true sharks but had jaws and a lateral line similar to modern sharks.

● **By about 360 mya**, sharks of many shapes and sizes had developed. It was the golden age of sharks.

● **One of the earliest sharks** was *Cladoselache*, which lived about 370 mya. It was 1.5 m in length and had a powerful tail, like a modern mako shark.

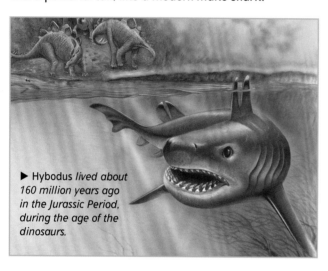

▶ Hybodus *lived about 160 million years ago in the Jurassic Period, during the age of the dinosaurs.*

● ***Stethacanthus***, which lived about 350 mya, had a helmet of small teeth on its head and a spiny brush sticking out of its back. This may have been used during courtship or for defence.

● ***Tristychius* was similar** to a modern dogfish, but lived about 350 mya. It had a spine on each dorsal fin.

● **The unicorn shark**, *Falcatus*, had an L-shaped spine on top of its head. Only males had this spine, which may have been used to fight rival males or to attract females.

● **The whorl-tooth shark**, *Helicoprion*, did not lose its teeth. They moved along in a spiral and then were stored in a special chamber under its bottom jaw.

● **The giant scissor-toothed shark**, *Edestus giganteus*, had a mouth one metre wide. Its teeth were replaced in rows, but the old teeth stuck out in front of the shark's head and did not fall out.

● **About 150 mya**, sharks of the golden age began to die out. The ancestors of modern sharks, which were fast-swimming hunters, began to take over.

● **The biggest shark** was probably *Megalodon* from 20 mya. It was 20 m in length (as long as two buses).

Shark fossils

● **Fossils are the remains** of, or the shape of, an animal preserved in rock. Often only the hardest parts of an animal, such as its skeleton, become fossilized.

● **When an animal dies**, its flesh and other soft parts start to rot. The harder parts, such as bone, rot more slowly and last longer. Over time, sediment layers settle on the remains. Minerals and salts replace the once-living parts and turn them and the sediments into solid rock.

● **As sharks have soft skeletons** made from cartilage, there are few whole shark fossils.

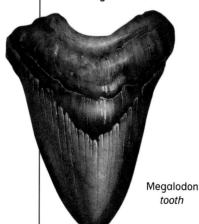

▼ *Fossilized teeth have shown us that* Megalodon *was much bigger than hunting sharks today.*

Megalodon
tooth

Great white shark tooth

● **Scientists use shark fossils** to find out what sharks looked like long ago and how they lived. They often use tooth fossils to guess how big an entire shark was.

● **Shark fossils** are often found on land in places that used to be seas millions of years ago.

● **Some of the best shark fossil areas** are in parts of the United States, such as California, Maryland and Oklahoma.

● **Fossils of *Cladoselache***, one of the earliest known sharks, have been found with fish preserved in their stomachs.

● **Fossil shark teeth** are common because ancient sharks shed many teeth in a lifetime, like living sharks. Shark teeth are as hard as human teeth and do not rot away.

● **Fossil teeth** from relatives of today's mackerel sharks, such as ancient porbeagle sharks, have been found in rocks dating back 100 million years.

● **Fossil *Megalodon* teeth** date from over 15 mya ago to less than 2 mya.

Sharks in trouble

● **Shark populations are falling** mainly because of human activities, such as hunting, overfishing and the use of shark body parts in medicine.

● **Humans catch** over 100 million sharks every year, perhaps as many as 250 million.

● **Some shark species**, such as the spotted wobbegong, are still hunted for their skin. It is made into items such as belts, wallets, shoes and handbags.

● **Shark liver oil** has traditionally been used to waterproof boats, for lighting, cosmetics, paint, machine oil and as a source of Vitamin A in health supplements.

● **Sharks caught for sport** are usually released, but often die from exhaustion soon afterwards.

● **Sharks mature slowly** and don't always bear many young, so it can be hard for a species to build up their numbers again after being overfished.

● **Sharks are at the top of the food chain.** Poisonous chemicals from pollution collect in sea creatures, which the sharks eat. The poison then builds up in the sharks' bodies. Scientists think this may make sharks ill and make it harder for them to reproduce.

▲ *Many sharks die when they become tangled up in fishing or safety nets.*

● **Some sharks** live near the coast and young sharks often use shallow coastal waters as nursery areas. These areas are regularly polluted by human sewage and other waste, as well as by agricultural and industrial chemicals washed into the sea from rivers.

● **The demand for shark fin soup** in parts of Asia is responsible for the deaths of millions of sharks every year, including hammerheads, which have large fins.

● **The fins may be removed** from the shark, which is then thrown back into the sea while still alive. The shark dies soon afterwards because it can't get enough oxygen to breathe or hunt for food. This cruel practice is banned in about one third of shark-fishing countries.

Endangered species

● **An endangered species** is in danger of dying out completely and becoming extinct.

● **Scientists try to find out** if a shark species is at risk by counting sharks seen in a particular area and measuring how much this changes over time.

● **Experts found** that sandbar shark sightings on America's east coast fell by 20 percent over 20 years. This shark is now classed as vulnerable.

● **Overfishing is the main reason** that sharks become endangered.

▼ *Even though basking sharks are protected in some parts of the world, these large sharks are still at risk because they grow and mature slowly, and take a long time to reproduce.*

● **International organizations** such as the IUCN (International Union for the Conservation of Nature and Natural Resources) compile lists of endangered species to raise awareness.

● **According to the IUCN** over 50 shark species are now endangered, and 30 percent of sharks and rays are threatened with extinction in the wild. Several species of sawfish are critically endangered and may die out soon.

● **Great whites**, whale sharks, basking sharks, makos, porbeagles and threshers are just a few of those at risk.

● **More than half** of all angelshark species are threatened with extinction because they are overfished.

● **Some sharks are threatened** when natural coastlines and estuaries are developed and built on. This destroys nurseries where sharks lay eggs or bear young.

● **Some of the rarest sharks** are river sharks, the daggernose shark and several species of angelshark. Several deep-water sharks, including the gulper shark and Harrisson's dogfish, are also vulnerable.

Saving sharks

◀ *A respected advocate for shark management, the Shark Trust is part of a global collaborative movement in shark conservation. It works to safeguard shark, skate and ray populations through science, education, influence and action.*

● **Ecotourism helps** to save sharks by encouraging local people not to kill them, as they can make money from sharks as tourist attractions.

● **Some shark-fishing** countries have imposed quotas to limit how many sharks fishermen can catch.

● **Governments can ban** the killing of some sharks altogether.

● **The UK has passed a law** making it illegal to catch or disturb a basking shark.

● **Some countries** have set up marine wildlife reserves where hunting wildlife is banned.

● **Conservation charities** such as the WWF (World Wildlife Fund) and Shark Trust work to educate people to help them avoid killing sharks unnecessarily.

● **By banning trade** in shark products, governments can help to stop unnecessary killing of sharks.

● **To help protect sharks**, people should avoid buying products such as shark fin soup.

● **Modern aquariums** and sea life centres help to explain the importance of shark conservation to their visitors. They also look after injured sharks, which can be returned to the wild when they recover.

● **Many sharks** could be saved from extinction if we work towards keeping the oceans clean and free of pollution, and try to preserve important shark habitats, such as coral reefs, near the shore.

● **More scientific** research into sharks would help us to better understand their biology and behaviour, and work out the best ways of helping sharks to survive in the future.

▼ *Tourists line up to take close-up photographs of blacktip reef sharks. The sharks have learned that they will get a free meal of fish if they swim in this area.*

Index

Entries in **bold** refer to main entries; entries in *italics* refer to illustrations.

African sawtail catsharks 45
ampullae of Lorenzini 11, 20, *20*, 51
anal fins 12, *12*, 34, 36
angelsharks 4, 12, 13, 14, 21, 34, **35**, *35*, 52, 61
Atlantic weasel sharks 46
attack behaviour 22, 41, 47
attacks on humans
  sharks 4, 7, 40, 42, 44, 48, **58**
  stingrays 53

backbones 15, *15*
bait balls *21*, 22
balance 10, 12, 19
balloonsharks *see* swellsharks
bamboo sharks 19, 28, 29, 38
barbels 14, 19, 35, *35*, 39, 40, 46
bareskin dogfish 37
barnacles 31
basking sharks 6, 7, 10, 23, 26, 29, 31, 40, **43**, *43*, 61, *61*, 62
bat rays 46
batoids 4, 52
benthic sharks 6
bigeye thresher sharks 4, 42
bighead catsharks 45
bioluminescence 4, 6, 26, 36, 37
birth **29**
  see also pups
blacknose sharks 7
blacktip reef sharks 7, 10, *18*, 22, *28*, 29, **49**, *49*, 58, *62*
blind sharks 38
blue sharks 4, *4*, 7, *10*, 11, *11*, 19, 26, 27, 29, *29*, 30, **47**, *47*
blue whales 23
blue-spotted stingrays *53*
bluntnose sixgill sharks *6*
body language 7, 10, 26
bonnethead sharks *12*, 29, 51, *51*
Borneo river sharks 50
bowmouth guitarfish 54
box jellyfish *58*
brains 10, 15, *15*, 18, 19, 20
bramble sharks 13, *13*
breathing 10
bronze whaler sharks *21*
bull sharks 4, 6, *6*, 21, 26, 47, *47*, **48**, *48*, 58

bullhead sharks 4, 10, 28, 34, **38**, *38*

camouflage 7, *13*, **14**, *14*, 35, 37, 38, *45*, 47, 49, 54
cannibalism 21, 26, 30, 42, 48
captive sharks 20, 42, 43, 45, 59
Caribbean reef sharks 7, 58
carpet sharks 13, 20, 21, 34, **38**, *38*, 40
cartilage 15, *15*, 52
catsharks 6, 14, 28, *28*, **45**, *45*
caudal fins 12, *12*
chain sharks 45
chimaeras 28, 52, **55**
Cladoselache 60
claspers 27, 28
classification **34**
cleaner wrasse 31
'cleaning stations' 31
coffin rays 53
cold water sharks 6, 7
cold-bloodedness 15
collared carpet sharks 38
common thresher sharks 4, 42
communication 7, 10, **26**, 37
conservation **62**
cookie-cutter sharks 4, 6, *6*, 14, **37**, *37*
copepods 31, *31*, 36
coral catsharks *45*
countershading 14, 47
cow sharks 34
cownose rays 53
crested bullhead sharks *38*
crocodile sharks 41

daggernose sharks 61
deep-water sharks 6, 18, 19, 23, 36, 37, 46, 50, 61
defences **14**
denticles 13, *13*, 28, 37
diving cages 59, *59*
dogfish sharks 4, 6, 7, 11, 14, 21, 22, *22*, 23, 26, 27, 28, 29, 30, 34, **36**, *36*, 37, 45, 58, 61
dorsal fins 12, *12*, 34, 45, 47, 50, 51
draughtsboard sharks 45
duckbilled rays 53
dusky sharks 29
dwarf lanternsharks 5
dwarf sharks 6

eagle rays 53
ears 19
ecotourism 62
Edestus giganteus 60
egg cases 28, *28*, 38, 45, 54, 55
egg sacs 29, *29*

eggs
  chimaeras 28, 55
  laying **28**
  rays 52
  sharks 4, 10, 27, 28, 38, 45
  skates 28, 54
elasmobranchology 59
electric rays 14, **53**, *53*
electrical sense 20, 41, 50
elephant fish 55, *55*
epaulette sharks 12, 14, 34, *38*
eyes 4, 6, **18**, 31, 36, 42, 47, 48, 49, 50, *50*
  chimaeras 55

Falcatus 60
feeding frenzy 22
female sharks 27, **28**, 29
fighting 7, 26
filter-feeding 5, 21, **23**, *23*, 39, 40, 41, 43
fins
  rays 52
  sharks 6, 10, 11, **12**, *12*, 13, 40, 61
  see also anal fins; caudal fins; dorsal fins; pectoral fins; pelvic fins
flapper skates 54, *54*
food and feeding 4, 5, 6, **21**, 39
  filter-feeding 5, 21, **23**, *23*, 39, 40, 41, 43
  scavenging **23**
fossils **60**, *60*
freshwater sharks 47, 48, 50
frilled sharks 6, *6*, 13, 29, 34

Galapagos sharks 10, 38, 58
gall bladder *15*
Ganges sharks 50
ghost catsharks 45
ghost sharks 52
ghouls 52
giant guitarfish 54
giant hammerhead sharks 21
giant lanternsharks 5
gill rakers 23
gills 15, 35, 47, *49*, 55
goblin sharks 6, *6*, 13, 34, 40, **41**, *41*
golden cow-nosed rays 52
granular dogfish 37
great hammerhead sharks *6*, 51, 58
great white sharks 4, 5, 7, 11, 12, *12*, 18, 19, 20, 21, 22, 23, 26, 30, 40, 42, **43**, *43*, 52, 58, *59*, 61
green dogfish 37
green sawfish 55
Greenland sharks 4, 6, 7, *7*, 23, 30, 31, *31*, **36**, *36*

grey reef sharks 7, *12*, 19, 26, 58
ground sharks 34
groups (packs) of sharks 7, 20, 22, **26**, 36, 40, 42, 43, 46, 51
guitarfish 4, 14, 52, **54**, *54*
gulf wobbegong sharks *40*
gulper sharks 6, 36, 61
gummy sharks 46

habitat destruction 55, 61
habitats **6–7**, 10, 62
hammerhead sharks 5, 6, 7, 13, *18*, 20, 21, **26**, 29, **51**, *51*, 58, 61
Harrisson's dogfish 61
hearing **19**
heart 15, *15*
Helicoprion 60
hooktooth sharks 46
horn sharks 7, 10, *12*, 28, 38, 58
houndsharks **46**, *46*
hunting **22**, 26, 30, 42
Hybodus 60

intelligence **20**
Irrawaddy river sharks 50

Japanese angelsharks 35
Japanese sawsharks 35

kitefin sharks 36

lampreys 31
lanternsharks 5, 6, 36, **37**, *37*
large-tooth cookie-cutter sharks 37
large-tooth sawfish 55
lateral line 19, *19*
Latin names 34
leaping 4, 11, 22, 43
lemon sharks 15, 20, *20*, 22, 26, 27, 29, *29*, 30, 31, 47, *48*
leopard sharks 14, *14*, 46
leopard whiprays 52
lesser electric rays 53, *53*
lifespans 4, 30, 39, 43, 44
lined lanternsharks 37
livers 10, 15, *15*, 29, 39, 41, 43
lollipop catsharks 45
long-tailed carpet sharks 38
longfin mako sharks 44
longnose sawsharks 35

mackerel sharks 6, 34, **40**, 43
mako sharks 4, 6, *6*, 7, 11, *11*, 12, 29, 30, 40, 42, **44**, *44*, 58, 61
mandarin dogfish *6*
manta rays 5, 31, 52

marbled catsharks 14
marbled electric rays 53
mating 11, 26, **27**, 30, 47
Megalodon 5, 60, *60*
megamouth sharks 12, 23, 40, **41**, *41*
migrations 7, **11**, 18, 40, 44, 46, 49
monkfish *see* angelsharks
movement, constant 10

navigation 11
New Guinea river sharks 50
nictitating eyelids 18, 34, 46, 47
night sharks **50**, *50*
nocturnal sharks 18, 22, 39
noises 26, 39, 45
nurse sharks 6, 7, 12, 19, 21, 26, 27, 29, 38, **39**, *39*, 58
nursery areas 26, 30, 61

oceanic whitetip sharks 7, 18, 58
ocellated angelsharks 35
olfactory lobes 18
overfishing 40, 47, 55, 61
oviparous sharks 28
ovoviviparous rays 52
ovoviviparous sharks 29

Pacific sleeper sharks 36
parasites 31
pectoral fins 12, *12*, 26, 50, 51, 52, 54
pelagic sharks 6
pelagic stingrays 52, 53
pelagic thresher sharks 42
pelvic fins 12, *12*, 28
pheromones 26, 27
photophores 37, *37*
pilotfish 31
pineal eye 18
Pinocchio catsharks 45
plankton 21, 23, 26, 39, 52
play behaviour 44
poisonous flesh 4, 36
pollution 19, 61, 62
porbeagle sharks 6, 7, 12, 40, *40*, **44**, *44*, 58, 60, 61
Port Jackson sharks 6, 14, *21*, 38
Portuguese sharks 6
precaudal pit *46*
predators 14
pregnancies 29, 36, 39, 42, 43, 44, 46, 49, 51
prehistoric sharks 5, **60**
prickly sharks 6
pups
  guitarfish 54
  rays 53
  sawfish 55

pups (*cont.*)
  sharks 4, 11, 26, *28*, **29**, *29*, 30, 35, 36, 39, 40, 42, 43, 44, 46, 47, 48, 49, 50, 51
pygmy sharks 5, *5*, 22, 36

ratfish 52
rays 4, 5, 14, 31, 46, **52–53**, *52*, *53*, 54, 58
reef sharks **7**, *7*, 10, *12*, 18, 19, 22, 26, 27, *27*, *28*, 47, 49, 58
remora fish 31, *31*
requiem sharks 6, **47**
resting 10, 26, *27*, 45
river sharks 4, 47, **50**, 61
river stingrays 53
rostrums 35, 55
roughsharks 14, 36
round stingrays 53

salmon sharks 11, 40
sand sharks 29
sand tiger sharks 10, 22, 26, 29, **42**, *42*, 58
sandbar sharks 61
sawfish 4, 52, *52*, **55**, *55*, 61
sawsharks 6, 13, 14, 19, 34, **35**, *35*
scalloped hammerhead sharks 7, 20, 51
scavenging **23**, 36
scissor-toothed sharks 60
sea leeches 31
senses **18–20**, 22
sevengill sharks 6
shark meat 4, 36
shark products, trade in 61, 62
Shark Trust 62
sharkfin guitarfish *see* bowmouth guitarfish
sharks
  anatomy **15**, *15*
  carnivores 4
  characteristics 4
  classification **34**
  conservation **62**
  endangered 4, 50, **61**
  fossils **60**, *60*
  growth and maturation 30
  habitats 4, **6–7**, 10
  intelligence **20**
  lifespans 4, 30, 39, 43, 44
  male and female **28**
  prehistoric 5, **60**
  records and statistics **4**
  relatives **52**
  senses **18–20**, 22
  shapes **13**
  size **5**
  species of 4, **34**
  study of sharks **59**, 62
  swimming skills **10**, 12, 14

short-nose electric rays 53
short-tail nurse sharks 39
shortfin mako sharks 4, 11, *11*, 40, 44, 58
shovelnose guitarfish 14, 54, *54*
shy-eye sharks 18
sicklefin weasel sharks 21, 46
silky sharks *13*, 22
silvertip sharks 7
sixgill sawsharks 35
sixgill sharks 6, *6*
skates 4, 28, 52, **54**, *54*
skin 11, **13**, *13*, 14, 27, 37, 47, 61
sleeper sharks 6, 7, 36
smalleye pygmy sharks 36
smalltooth sawfish *52*
smell, sense of **18**
smooth dogfish 23
smooth hammerhead sharks **51**, *51*
smoothhound sharks 7, 21, 46
snaggletooth sharks 46
snouts 13, 22, 26, 34, 35, 38, 39, 40, 41, *41*, 49, 50
solitary sharks 26
speartooth sharks 50, *50*
speed 4, **11**, 12, 48
sperm 27, 28
spined pygmy sharks 5
spines 14, 36, 38, 55, 58, 60
  rays 53
spinner sharks **49**, *49*
spiny dogfish 4, 6, 7, 14, 22, *22*, 26, 29, 36, 46
spiracles 19, 35
spitting sharks *see* tawny nurse sharks
spongehead catsharks 45
spook fish 52
sport fishing 44, 61
spotted eagle rays 53
spotted houndsharks *46*
spotted wobbegong sharks 40, 61
Stethacanthus 60
stingrays 52, **53**, *53*, 58
study of sharks **59**, 62
swellsharks 14, 26, 28, **45**, *45*
swimming skills **10**, 12, 14
symbiotic relationships 31

tagging sharks 59
tails 4, *4*, 10, **12**, *12*, 14, 26, 42, *42*
  rays 52
tapetum lucidum 18
tapeworms 31
tasselled wobbegong sharks *13*, 40
taste, sense of **19**
tawny nurse sharks 39

teeth and jaws
  chimaeras 55
  fossil teeth 60, *60*
  prehistoric sharks 60
  rays 53
  sharks 4, *15*, **21**, 22, 30, 31, 37, *37*, 38, 39, 41, 42, 44, 45, 46, 48, 49, 50
temperate water sharks 7
territories 10
Texas skates 54
threat displays 26, *26*
thresher sharks 4, *4*, 6, 12, *12*, 14, 29, 40, **42**, *42*, 61
tiger sharks 4, 6, *12*, 20, *20*, 21, *21*, 23, 29, 47, **48**, *48*
tope sharks 46
torpedo rays 52, 53
touch, sense of **19**
tracking sharks 59
Tristychius 60

unicorn sharks 60

velvet belly lanternsharks 6, 37
vertebrates 15
viper dogfish 37
vision **18**
viviparous sharks 29

warm water sharks 7
warm-bloodedness 43
weasel sharks **46**, *46*
whale sharks 4, 5, *5*, 6, *6*, 7, 12, *13*, 18, 23, *23*, 28, 29, 30, 31, 34, 38, **39**, *39*, 61
whaler sharks *see* requiem sharks
whiskery sharks 46
white sharks 18
whitespotted bamboo sharks 29
whitetip reef sharks 7, 10, *10*, 22, 26, 27, *27*, 49
whorl-tooth sharks 60
winghead sharks 5, 51
wobbegong sharks 4, 13, *13*, 14, 19, 28, 38, **40**, *40*, 58, 61

zebra sharks 14, 28, 29, 38, 39